living pg. 52

How to live on Alexanderplatz. Along with the city's most glamorous hotel suites and best youth hostels.

culture pg. 62

Viva VJ Enie on the prowl for men and art treasures. And an overview of the blooming cultural landscape.

sports pg. 74

The Berlin basketball team "Albatross" flying to the net, the best places to jog, and some shopping tips for sporting goods.

sightseeing pg. 84

A thumbnail guide to cool architecture, spectacular castles, and a great view of the city from the water.

PHOTOS: Daniela Eger Z21 , Kerstin Ehmer, Barbi & Jan, Jürgen Holzenleuchter, Manuel Krug, Steffen Jänicke, Poolfoto/Horizon

Max

Riding Berlin for under 8 marks

Taking public transportation in Berlin without a ticket? It's a nerve-wracking experience, and it doesn't cost much to avoid it.

Berliners like to complain about the BVG (the public transport system) even though trains and buses are frequent and dependable. Some of them even run all night long. For a mere DM 3.90 you can ride for two hours, and for DM 7.80 you can ride all day. Riding without a ticket is free of course, but if you're caught you will have to pay a hefty fine of DM 60. Pay cash on the spot if possible (because the BVG will threaten to report you to the police if you are caught twice). Riding ticketless on either the U-Bahn (the subway) or the longer-distance S-Bahn trains is pretty risky, but it's a little safer on buses. If you're caught and the inspectors ask to see your ticket, act calm and friendly, and maybe you can escape by just showing an old stub!

Berlin by the

Important statistics about the capital.

Cultural

3.36 million people live in Berlin, which averages out to 3,900 people per square kilometer. The total area of the city is 391.7 square kilometers.

Social

There is only one doctor for every 548 people in Berlin, but the ratio of dogs to people is a little more balanced, with one dog for every 35 humans. Additionally, Berlin has 68.5 hectares of land for growing vegetables, but an inordinate amount of this land is used to grow parsely (12 hectares, to be exact).

Older than its big brother

Talk about the new capital leaves the village of Berlin cold.

Its 480 inhabitants have other things to worry about: for example, no one obeys the 30 kilometers per hour speed limit! Tips for people who want to visit: the village is part of the municipality of Seedorf and is on the border of Holsteinische Schweiz, about 80 kilometers from Hamburg. The metropolis of Berlin is 357 kilometers away, but the residents of the village are very proud that the place where they live is officially nineteen years older than its big brother.

Numbers

Criminal
In Berlin last year the police hotline was called a total of 881,000 times for 445 cases of exhibitionism, 6,373 cases of falsified documents, and 1,450 cases of people dodging restaurant or bar bills.

Animal
In 1994 there were almost 1,500 sheep grazing in Berlin's meadows. By 1996 there were only 517 of them left. Does this mean there are no more sheep left in Berlin? With 137 official cases of poaching in 1998, this seems to be a logical conclusion.

PHOTOS: Jörg Lehmann (4), Markus Weber (1)

Poison center
Tel. 192 40

Pharmacies
Hours change at different locations, so consult the web:
www.citylive.de/aponodie/be/apolist.htm

AIDS hotline
Tel. 194 11

Drug-related emergencies
Tel. 192 37

Psychological help
Women's crisis line
Tel. 625 42 43
Crisis line
Tel. 111 03

Hotline for children
Tel. 61 00 61

Lost and found
Central lost and found
Tel. 69 93 64 44
Lost and found for the BVG (public transport)
Tel. 25 62 30 40
Lost and found for Deutsche Bahn (trains)
Tel. 29 72 96 12

Religious hotline
Tel. 111 01

Help for crime victims
Tel. 395 28 67

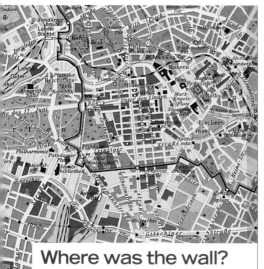

Where was the wall?

Despite rumors to the contrary, the Berlin Wall still exists. Tips for people who want to have a look:

The Berliners did a thorough job: ten years ago the "woodpeckers" managed to reduce 107.3 kilometers of cement wall, watchtowers, and tank obstacles to rubble. Most of the material went to collectors around the world or was used to build roads. Nevertheless, you can still find sections of the wall on the borders of Kreuzberg, Treptow, and Friedrichshain. The last watchtower is at Schlesicher Busch, and since 1992, it has been a museum for banned art. If you are looking for a bigger stretch of wall, go to the East Side Gallery (Mühlenstrasse), the largest open-air gallery in the world. Near Brandenburger Tor, white crosses commemorate the people who died trying to cross the wall. Finally, head for Checkpoint Charlie on Friedrichstrasse and see history come to life.

Recycling and Gloss

The city magazines *Tip* and *Zitty* are published every fourteen days. Both provide a comprehensive overview of cultural events and the party scene, and also include large classified sections. Which one you choose is a matter of taste. *Tip* (DM 4.50), published in a glossy format, offers extensive cultural reviews, while *Zitty* (DM 4) has a more alternative feel—it is published on recycled paper and favors articles on political and social issues.

He made a good showing, but ultimately didn't make the list: Leonard Cohen with "First We Take Manhattan, then we take Berlin."

Glockenturm
(Near Olympiastadion)
Tel. 23 08 82 30

Deep in the Ravine
The Waldbühne stadium is enormous—but still cozy.

The Waldbühne stadium has been drawing crowds for sixty-three years. Located deep in a ravine, it can accommodate more than twenty thousand spectators. Used initially for boxing matches, it became instantly famous when a Rolling Stones concert held here in 1965 ended in rioting. In 1981 Berliner Peter Schwenkow took on its management and, step by step, transformed it into one of the most popular venues in Germany.

Top ten

Music

1. **Heroes**
   David Bowie
2. **Berlin, Berlin**
   Harald Juhnke
3. **Auf'm Bahnhof Zoo
   [At the Zoo Station]**
   Nina Hagen
4. **Rauchhaus Song
   [Smoke House Song]**
   Ton, Steine, Scherben
5. **(Ich steh auf) Berlin [(I
   have a fancy for) Berlin]**
   Ideal
6. **Kreuzberger Nächte
   [Kreuzberger Nights]**
   Gebrüder Blattschuß
7. **Sonderzug nach
   Pankow [A Special Train
   to Pankow]**
   Udo Lindenberg
8. **The Wall**
   Westbam
9. **Halloween in Ostberlin
   [Halloween in East Berlin]**
   Silly
10. **Walls Come Tumbling
    Down**
    Style Council

Film

1. **One, Two, Three**
   Billy Wilder
2. **Himmel Über Berlin
   (Wings of Desire)**
   Wim Wenders
3. **Run Lola Run**
   Tom Tykwer
4. **Der blaue Engel (The
   Blue Angel)**
   Josef von Sternberg
5. **Christiane F.**
   Uli Edel
6. **Life is a Construction
   Site**
   Wolfgang Becker
7. **Aimée and Jaguar**
   Max Färberböck
8. **Richy Guitar**
   Die Ärzte
9. **Wir Kellerkinder (We
   Basement Kids)**
   Wolfgang Neuss
10. **Querelle**
    R. W. Fassbinder

Books

1. **Berlin Alexanderplatz**
   Alfred Döblin
2. **Emil and the Detectives**
   Erich Kästner
3. **Summerhouse, Later**
   Judith Hermann
4. **The Innocent**
   Ian McEwan
5. **Berlin Noir**
   Philip Kerr
6. **Goodbye to Berlin**
   *Christopher
   Isherwood*
7. **Der Hauptmann von
   Köpenick (The Captain
   from Köpenick)**
   Carl Zuckmayer
8. **Paarungen [Pairings]**
   Peter Schneider
9. **Potsdamer Ableben
   (Death in Potsdam)**
   Pieke Biermann
10. **Wo liegt Berlin?
    (Where is Berlin?)**
    Alfred Kerr

Books

Everything you need to know about Berlin trends in fifty-five lessons—from the enthusiasm for balloon-silk track suits to the fanatic love of animals: *How do I become a Berliner?* by Carmen Böker and Silvia Meixner.

Observations from outside the mainstream about culture, sports, ethics, and the media show that Berlin is: *The Turbulent City* by Thomas Krüger.

A lexical overview of Berlin's best art, with more than six hundred entries: *Berlin Culture Handbook* by Klaus von Siebenhaar.

New Year's Eve 2000

Expectations are high. Will there be two million visitors? The biggest party in the city will be at Brandenburger Tor. SAT 1 will broadcast live, just like they did last year. More than two hundred bands, stars, and other important people will be there, and at the end there will be the biggest fireworks display of all time. But that's not all. Unesco is celebrating the turn of the millennium in Berlin; in the ICC conference center there will be a gigantic party with music and theater; the Hotel Palace is offering opulent packages for the celebration; and there will be a special performance at the Konzerthaus. And where will the chancellor be? Doing what politicians do best, Gerhard Schröder will speak before the Reichstag. For more information: Tel. 24 60 32 52.

The Train is Coming (to Berlin)

Train stations are about to undergo a transformation into nice places to while away one's leisure time. At least, this is what Germany's railway system hopes as it invests billions in the project. A scenario for Berlin's future:

The times when travelers had to rush through dark, stuffy halls are a thing of the past. Deutsche Bahn AG, the German rail system, is spending extravagantly to redesign its stations in the capital: ten modern travel centers are planned. The Lehrter Bahnhof is first on the list. At a cost of DM 800 million, Deutsche Bahn is building Europe's largest railway junction in the middle of the Tiergarten. The main hall will be 430 meters long, with a glass canopy, a subterranean switching system, and five levels for trains.

Golf

Golf is not known for being a cheap sport and it's unheard of to play for free—unless you're in Berlin. Motto: "Volksgolf." On the former grounds of the Stadion der Weltjugend (Stadium for the World's Youth), between the Schwartzkopffstrasse and Zinnowitzer Strasse subway stations, there is a place for driving and putting. A basket of balls costs only DM 3. The icing on this good deal: children do not have to pay for golf balls, and also receive free instruction.

Dance

Beginning at 6 p.m. on Mondays, female fans of the waltz and the cha-cha can dance for free, with a teacher, at the Begine Women's Center (Potsdamer Strasse 139, Tel. 21 54 23 25). Here's the catch: no men allowed!!

The Philharmonic

Whoever dreamed about taking a peep behind the scenes at an important cultural institution has that chance, every day at 1 p.m. The Philharmonic (Herbert-von-Karajan-Strasse 1, Tel. 25 48 80) offers free tours. Go to the service entrance and ask the porter.

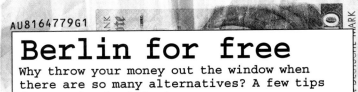

Berlin for free

Why throw your money out the window when there are so many alternatives? A few tips for people who like to save:

Museum

Art doesn't have to cost money. The German Guggenheim Museum (Unter den Linden 13-15, Tel. 202 09 30) and the Academy of Art (Hanseatenweg 10, Tel. 39 07 60) are free on Mondays from 11 a.m. to 8 p.m. Another tip: all state museums offer free admission on the first Sunday in every month.

Salon culture

Come on in—make yourself at home. In Juliette's literary salon (by the corner of Gormannstrasse and Linienstrasse) people sit around with art books and free coffee, discussing aesthetics, philosophy, and the world.

Climbing

The dream of all mountaineers stuck in the lowlands: a climbing wall. With a bonus view of the north. If you take the U-Bahn to the Voltastrasse Station, you can get to the ersatz mountain in Humboldthain in no time at all.

Calendar of Events

Summer

Long Night of the Museums
Thirty museums open their
doors to the public.

August 28, 1999

**International Broadcasting
Exhibition**
The biggest media fair in the
country. Loads of celebrities and
promotional gifts.

*August 28 –
September 5,
1999*

49th Berlin Festival Week
The central cultural event of the
Philharmonic. This year the focus
is the work of Gustav Mahler. For
more information: Tel. 25 48 90

*September 3-9,
1999*

Berlin Marathon
A sporting event with the spirit
of a public celebration.

*September 26,
1999*

Fall

art forum berlin
The most important art fair in
Germany, at the Exhibition
Center (Messegelände).
Tel. 303 80

*September
30–October 4,
1999*

Jazz Fest Berlin
At the Haus der Kulturen der
Welt, cool music.

*November 4–7,
1999*

Venus 99
International erotic trade fair.

*November
11–14, 1999*

Winter

Niklausmarkt
A Christmas market named in
honor of St. Nicholas, Christian
patron saint of children. At
Castle Charlottenburg.

*December 3–12,
1999*

Spring

Kurt Weill Fest
Festival in honor of the compos-
er, best known for his work with
Bertolt Brecht. For more information: Tel. 203 09 23 96

*March 2–April
3, 2000*

Some malicious
people say that
Berlin
is provincial.
But why
shouldn't they?
The
center is
actually the
meeting point
of nine
villages, which
together make
up the city. A
brief overview:

**Charlotten-
burg**
This is the nostal-
gia center of
West Berlin, with
a distinct allergy
for the east—no
other neighborhood
is as representative of
the period before the
tearing down of the
wall. And that retro
feeling lives on: the in-
habitants don't seem to
notice that the hipster sce
has long since moved east

Wilmersdorf

Good Neighbors

Reinickendorf

Weißensee

Pankow
Many displaced
Pankowers are
returning to
where they came
from, full of
nostalgia.

Wedding
Before 1989 Wedding was one of
the best-loved, and also one of
the liveliest, parts of the city. Since
then things have quieted down.
Müllerstrasse has become deserted,
with more and more of its small
shops standing empty.

**Prenzlauer
Berg**

This became the
city's "in" neighborhood
far too quickly. People who grew
up here are torn between their
hatred for tourists and their
reluctance to leave a truly
charming district.

garten
re the hectic ef-
s to move the
pital from Bonn got
nder way, this was a
pretty sleepy neigh-
borhood. The only
things that drew
people here were
Alt-Moabit, a
popular shopping
street, and, of
course, the park.

Mitte
Mitte is a great
place to work, study,
shop—and govern!
Places like the
Gendarmenmarkt are a must
for every sightseer, and the
Hakesche Höfe is the main
attraction in the evening.

**Fried-
richshain**
A big student
neighborhood,
with a little some-
thing extra. A
popular place to
go out, with lots
of trendy
bars and
cafés.

Kreuzberg
When the residents were still
throwing stones, hordes of tourists
came to watch. The tourists have since
moved east, and now the
Kreuzbergers have their nice
bars all to themselves again. .

Schöneberg
Many interest-
ing cafés, bars,
and shops,
often in beau-
tiful old build-
ings.

Tempelhof

Neukölln

New Media Center

Long a black hole on the map of the media world, Berlin is making a comeback. Six examples

Cécile Dütsch, Moderator

Dütsch, a native Berliner, fights her way through the city's clubs with her camera, but without any hipster pretensions. The jerky footage is shown on *Spy*, a TV program aimed at younger viewers, for whom she is the ultimate anchorwoman. (She had a brief turn as a moderator on the music channel Viva, but was disappointed, and has returned to the local scene, even making an appearance in a video of the music band Rammstein.) Dütsch doesn't consider herself a creative artist—just a gal taking advantage of the opportunities in Berlin. Whether she finds them with the group Flirt or in her identity as a pinup girl, in times both up and down, if you make any effort at all to learn about popular culture in Berlin, it's hard to miss Dütsch. (By the way, she's also a state-certified high school teacher!)

Johnny Haeusler, Web designer

Johnny Haeusler used to make regular stage appearances with his punk band Plan B, and also did a stint as the presenter of the *Soundgarden* show on Jugendradio Fritz. He's continued with his work on the radio, but has taken a break with his musical career. Now he spends most of his time in his loft in Kreuzberg, where he has set up headquarters for his internet business, defcom webdressing (www.defcom.de). He has recently made sites for the Lemonbabies, Fettes Brot, and the magazine *Park*. Haeusler's web design is definitely a refreshing change from the usual techno-trash.

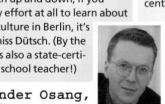

Alexander Osang, Reporter

Unlike many of his colleagues from the former East Germany, Alexander Osang writes *sans* any trace of sentimentality, without constantly having to remind everyone of how romantic it used to be to eat currywurst in Prenzlauer Berg. He knows the east, but doesn't show any formulaic solidarity with its people. And it wasn't long before he had the west figured out, too. Osang's profiles of important people are never cynical, but they spare no punches, either. His descriptions always seem to hit the mark. He has rejected offers from *Spiegel* and *Süddeutsche Zeitung*—one more thing that distinguishes him from his ambitious colleagues. Instead, he has stayed on as the head reporter for the *Berliner Zeitung*, a decision that Berliners should be grateful for.

Zucker.Kommunikation, Below-the-line promotions

An opportunity to generate buzz. That is how Oliver Kottwitz, Matthias Bonjer, and Michelle Nagel describe their line of work. So far they have done extremely well, and big clients like Sony, Levi's, and C & A come to them when they want to avoid a gigantic advertising campaign. When the agency organized a Levi's party in the Gedächtniskirche, managers from the American company were very impressed (especially since the Levi's logo was never used at all). The big accounts still go to traditional agencies, but there is still plenty of room for Zucker.Kommunikation to operate "below the line."

Sebastian Turner, Advertiser

For a long time advertisers used to see Berlin as a kind of diaspora. It still doesn't compare with Frankfurt or Hamburg, but a very promising state of affairs is slowly developing. Sebastian Turner was one of the pioneers, conquering the east for the agency Scholz & Friends, first in Hamburg and then in Berlin. Turner & Friends, who have their office in an old factory, have

launched many prize-winning campaigns, including one for the newspaper *FAZ*.

Gerhard Westrich, Photographer

When Gerhard Westrich packs up his gear, it looks like he's preparing for some kind of expedition! And this is a good description of how he sees his work. Westrich uses his camera to discover people and places. People you would usually pass on the street without noticing. Places that are in the neighborhood but still want to be discovered. Recently Westrich spent three weeks looking for religious communities in the city, and encountered coconut-smashing Hindus and Buddhists on a class trip through Brandenburger Tor. "A completely new world for me," Westrich said. And that's how people usually feel when they look at his pictures.

Battle for the Kiosks

A look at Berlin's most important newspapers

TV personality Giovanni di Lorenzo lured many star reporters to his paper in order to take on *Berliner Zeitung*. But there's a problem: *Der Tagesspiegel* is still seen as a West Berlin paper, and hardly anyone in the east bothers to look at it.
www.tagesspiegel.de

The *Berliner Morgenpost* is one hundred years old, and it's up to its editor-in-chief, Peter Philipps, to give it a facelift. So far he has done that, both discreetly and effectively. His goal: to hit the biggest subscription jackpot of any newspaper in Berlin.
www.berliner-morgenpost.de

Circulation king Franz Josef Wagner (of the paper known as *B2*) hasn't yet won the hearts of Berliners. But he's working twenty-five hours a day to do better!
www.bz-berlin.de

People have started to view *Berliner Zeitung* as a prestigious newspaper (a great achievement). The flip side: *Berliner Zeitung* is still seen as an East Berlin paper, and no one in the west seems to read it.
www.berlinonline.de

For years *Taz* has been able to survive by using ridiculous subscription promotions. It's still possible to find something good here—but mostly on the sports page.
www.taz.de

Many papers are slugging it out for readers among Berlin's 3.5 million inhabitants. The competition for circulation has clearly heated up recently, and all of them want to be what the *Washington Post* has become in America: *the* political rag.

Radio war

Over the past few years, radio has become less and less important. But there's a time of day when the radio is still hard to beat—those kick-start-the day hours between 6 a.m. and 9 a.m. During this short prime time the radio wakes people up, gets them singing in the shower, and accompanies them on their way to work, with news from world politics to traffic jams. Since this is the only time when there are enough listeners, it's also the only time when the stations make money. In Berlin, the hottest radio market in the country, competition has had some strange consequences—stations are constantly coming up with crazier and crazier contests to win listeners. Tune in early, and have fun.

Pixelpark

The online agency is Berlin's most successful multimedia venture

Paulus Neef is the head of Germany's leading agency in a new field: multimedia. Last year his on-line firm made DM 23 million, with clients from all different lines of business, ranging from electronics multi-national Siemens to singer Herbert Grönemeyer. Other clients include Bertelsmann, the media giant which, in addition to having Pixelpark build all its websites, also owns 75 percent of the company. Right now Pixelpark is planning to launch new branches in addition to current offices in Hamburg, Cologne, Stuttgart, New York, Basel, and Paris.

The friendly guide to electronics

In the spring of 1997, Sascha Kösch, Mercedes Bunz, and their colleagues had the idea that they would make a newspaper. Three months later the first issue was published. The *Zeitschrift für elektronische Lebensaspekte (Journal for the Electronic Aspects of Life)* covers a lot of territory, with topics ranging from electronic music to computer hard and software to social philosophy. For the first eighteen months the journal known as *Debug* didn't cost anything, but that changed in April 1999, when it went on sale at newsstands.

Alternative leaders
Some unusual publications

The first issue of *Style & The Family Tunes* appeared in 1993. The magazine covers fashion and music, and functions as a lively guide to pop culture. It has since been recognized as a "visual leader" and trendsetter throughout Germany. The art magazine *Shift* has positioned itself against commercialism of any kind. (It is also, ironically enough, so successful that it has become a popular item among collectors.)

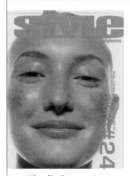

The listings magazine [030] is available for free in clubs and theaters. Published every fortnight, it has become the publication of choice for many Berliners trying to decide how to spend their leisure time.

PHOTO: Zinn (1)

For Sale!

KAISER'S COFFEE POT, PRICE: NEGOTIABLE

Almost two meters tall and made of red foam, the giant coffee pot spends most of its time on the rotary clothes-dryer in the garden. Christian Wagenbrecht, eight, is usually not allowed to wear it out onto the street. Besides, it's almost impossible to see anything when you have it on. Christian found Lupo, which is the coffee pot's proper name, at a neighbor's house in Hermannstrasse. Christian's mother has finally decided that, after hanging on the clothes-dryer for two years, Lupo needs to find a new home.

'60s GAS PUMP,
BUYER MUST REMOVE

Katharina Binder and Christian Wurster don't know how the gas pump got into their fifth floor walk-up apartment. All they know is that it was there when they moved in and that it weighs a ton. Now they want to leave, and the pump has got to go. They hope they will be able to find someone clever to dislodge it.

Zweite Hand, a newspaper consisting entirely of classified ads, is a bible for people either buying or selling second-hand goods. The paper offers an eccentric mix of curiosities, cult objects, and things people might actually have a use for. Motto: if it's good, it's good, if it's bad, it's better!

By Caroline von der Trann
Photos by Kerstin Ehmer

BOA CONSTRICTOR, TAME, DM 2,500 WITH TERRARIUM

Schali, a two meter-long boa, has been living with Thorsten Glaub for four years. But now Thorsten's girlfriend is moving in with him, and she doesn't like snakes. It's a shame, because Schali is actually the ideal house pet. Schali doesn't smell, doesn't make any noise, and only needs to be fed every four weeks. Disadvantage: the snake prefers to eat live animals.

TURKISH BELLY-DANCING COSTUME
NEW: DM 450, NOW: DM 250

Rosa Hoffmann caught belly-dancing fever ten years ago on a trip to Turkey. When she got back home, she bought a costume and took classes. She had a talent for it and soon she started getting bookings at restaurants. Later, when she was pregnant, she took a short break. But her ex-husband did not like being a babysitter. Now Rosa's son is eight years old and she is working as a city planner. But she doesn't intend to give up belly dancing: she actually has two more costumes in her closet.

HAT COLLECTION, PRICE: NEGOTIABLE

When Mariam Greese came to Berlin ten years ago she was immediately fascinated by the flea markets. At Winterfeldplatz she discovered a stand with all different kinds of hats. There was a particularly good one in a suitcase on the ground, and she bought it. Now she owns more than fifty hats, and wants to sell twelve of them.

Design for women

Prada

D 8 *Kurfürstendamm 189 (Charlottenburg); Uhlandstrasse subway station; Tel. 884 80 70; Monday through Friday 10 a.m. to 7 p.m., Saturday 10 a.m. to 4 p.m.; Amex, Visa, Master, Euro, Diners.*

The ultimate in women's fashion. A light sampling of different styles; the overall effect is perfection.

Modehaus Horn

D 8 *Kurfürstendamm 213 (Charlottenburg); Uhlandstrasse subway station; Tel. 881 40 55; Monday through Friday 10 a.m. to 7 p.m., Saturday 10 a.m. to 4 p.m.; Amex, Visa, Master, Euro, Diners.*

This feels like an ordinary

TRABANT, 1990, METALLIC GOLD-BROWN, PURPLE VELVET SEATS. PRICE: DM 1,900

Frank Langershausen didn't used to care much about cars. But that was before he met a new love in May 1995: the Trabant. Not having much money, he bought the car just to get around in, but now he is a member of a Trabant club. The car he owns was one of the last to roll off the assembly lines. But parting won't be difficult for him, as he has four more Trabants in the garage.

Charming and seductive: Prada

department store, but don't be fooled; an enormous smorgasbord of designers.

Claudia Skoda

E 7 *Kurfürstendamm 50 (Charlottenburg); Uhlandstrasse subway station; Tel. 885 10 09; Monday through Friday 11 a.m. to 7 p.m., Saturday 11 a.m. to 4 p.m.; Amex, Visa, Master, Euro.*

Skin-tight fabrics; some of the most beautiful clothing in Berlin.

Design for men and women

Kramberg

E 7 *Kurfürstendamm 56-57 (Charlottenburg); Uhlandstrasse subway station; Tel. 327 90 10; Monday through Wednesday 10 a.m. to 7 p.m., Thursday, Friday 10 a.m to 8 p.m., Saturday 10 a.m. to 4 p.m.; Amex, Euro, Visa, Master, Diners.*

One of the best selections of clothing in Berlin. Clothes by Armani and Calvin Klein, among others.

Jil Sander

D 8 *Kurfürstendamm 185 (Charlottenburg); Adenauerplatz subway station; Tel. 886 70 20; Monday through Friday 10 a.m. to 7 p.m., Saturday 10 a.m. to 4 p.m.; Amex, Visa, Master, Euro, Diners.*

The favorite designer for women who want to seduce with their intellects, and for men who like their clothing simple and elegant.

Donna Karan

I 7 *Friedrichstrasse 71 (Mitte); Stadtmitte subway station; Tel. 20 94 60 10; Monday through Friday 10 a.m. to 8 p.m., Saturday 10 a.m. to 4 p.m.; Amex, Visa, Master, Euro, Diners.*

DK fans no longer need to go to New York to pay homage to the Madonna of casual.

Gucci

I 7 *Friedrichstrasse 71 (Mitte); Stadtmitte subway station; Tel. 20 94 66 70; Monday through Friday 10 a.m. to 8 p.m., Saturday 10 a.m. to 4 p.m.; Amex, Visa, Master, Euro, Diners.*

The Gucci universe has found a base in the new upscale section of Mitte.

Versace Boutique

D 8 *Kurfürstendamm 185 (Charlottenburg); Uhlandstrasse subway station; Tel. 885 74 60; Monday through Friday 10 a.m. to 7 p.m., Saturday 10 a.m. to 4 p.m.; Amex, Visa, Master, Euro, Diners.*

Very Versace on two floors: Versace Couture, Versace Home Collection, and Versace Jewelery.

Elegant handbags: Jil Sander

Design for men

Patrik Hellmann

E 7/8 *Fasanenstrasse 29 (Charlottenburg); Uhlandstrasse subway station; Tel. 88 48 77 71; Monday through Friday 10 a.m. to 7 p.m., Thursday 10 a.m. to 8 p.m., Saturday 9:30 a.m. to 4 p.m.; Amex, Visa, Master, Euro.*

International designers and Patrik Hellmann's own collection (good value for the money).

Studio 2002

D 7 *Schlüterstrasse 26 (Charlottenburg); Uhlandstrasse subway station; Tel. 323 90 77; Monday through Friday 10 a.m. to 8 p.m., Saturday 10 a.m. to 4 p.m.; Amex, Visa, Master, Euro, Diners.*

The usual suspects like Hugo, D&G, and DSquared. Hip, but no hop.

Young designers

Molotow

I 8 *Gneisenaustrasse 112 (Kreuzberg); Mehringdamm subway station; Tel. 693 08 18; Monday through Friday 2 p.m. to 8 p.m., Saturday 12 noon to 4 p.m.; Visa, Euro, Amex, Diners.*

Molotow offers high-quality fashion for men and women. Newcomers appear side by side with established designers.

Tagebau

J 5 *Rosenthaler Strasse 19 (Mitte); Hackescher Markt S-Bahn station; Tel. 28 39 08 90; Monday through Saturday 11 a.m. to 8 p.m.; no credit cards.*

Six ambitious designers offer their

creations and all items are one of a kind.

Shoes

Budapester Schuhe
I 6 *Friedrichstrasse 81 (Mitte); Französische Strasse subway station; Tel. 20 38 81 10; Monday through Friday 10 a.m. to 8 p.m., Saturday 10 a.m. to 4 p.m. Amex, Visa, Master, Euro, Diners.*

Classic shoes for people who are willing to pay top prices. In the same building there is another shop offering more fashionable shoes for slightly younger people.

Von T.
D 7 *Bleibtreustrasse 27 (Charlottenburg); Savignyplatz S-Bahn station; Tel. 881 26 02; Monday through Friday 11 a.m. to 7 p.m., Saturday 10 a.m. to 4 p.m.; Visa, Amex, Master, Euro, Diners.*

Elegant selection of shoes by Dieter Kuckelhorn and classic English shoes by Edward Green. Prices are high, but not inappropriately so.

Schuhmacherei
I 9 *Bergmannstrasse 30 (Kreuzberg); Gneisenaustrasse subway station; Tel. 692 35 70; Monday through Friday 8 a.m. to 6:30 p.m., Saturday 10*

a.m. to 2 p.m.; all credit cards.
Genuine handmade shoes. You can be measured here for a custom pair.

Tizian
D 8 *Kurfürstendamm 187 (Charlottenburg); Uhlandstasse subway station; Tel. 88 50 01 80; Monday through Friday 10 a.m. to 8 p.m., Saturday 10 a.m. to 4 p.m.; Amex, Visa, Master, Euro, Diners.*

Masterpieces for men and women: Tods, Armani, Joop, Rossi, Boss, Hobson's, and Allen Edmonds.

Streets for shopping

It's nice when shops are close together—it spares shoe leather. Here you'll find many things you were not even looking for.

1. CHARLOTTENBURG
Kurfürstendamm
West Berlin's favorite shopping mile. Exclusive boutiques like Jil Sander, Claudia Skoda, and Versace. But also more egalitarian chains like H&M. An enormous selection of food. The Ku'damm and its side streets have everything you could possibly want.

2. MITTE
Friedrichstrasse
Berlin's other chic street for shopping. Next to Galeries Lafayette you'll find Kaufhaus Quartier 206, which lights up with international style. Boutiques of prestigious designers like Donna Karan, Etro, and Donna e Uomo compete for affluent customers.

3. SCHÖNEBERG
Maassenstrasse/ Winterfeldtstr./ Goltzstrasse
An interesting mix of small shops, boutiques offering fashion outside the mainstream, and nice cafés. Antiques, gourmet foods, and fine wines are well represented. Be sure not to miss the Winterfeldtmarkt, an outdoor market.

The top designers: Tizian

Groopie Deluxe
G 8/9 *Goltzstrasse 39 (Schöneberg) Eisenacher Strasse subway station; Tel. 217 20 38; Monday through Friday 11 a.m. to 8 p.m., Saturday 11 a.m. to 4 p.m.; all credit cards.*

Casual clubwear and bright wigs to add color to your life.

The Original Levi's Store
D 7/8 *Kurfürstendamm 237 (Charlottenburg); Kurfürstendamm subway station; Tel. 88 55 38 98; Monday through Friday 10 a.m. to 8 p.m., Saturday 10 a.m. to 4 p.m.; Amex, Visa, Master, Euro.*

Everything by Levi's on two and a half floors. What more could you want?

Diesel
E 7 *Kurfürstendamm 17 (Charlottenburg); Kurfürstendamm subway station; Tel. 88 55 14 53; Monday through Friday 10 a.m. to 8 p.m., Saturday 10 a.m. to 4 p.m.; Amex, Visa, Master.*

Enormous selection for fans of the hottest label in the schoolyard.

Maassen Zehn
G 8 *Maassenstrasse 10 (Schöneberg); Nollendorfplatz subway station; Tel. 215 54 56; Monday through Friday 10 a.m. to 7 p.m., Saturday 9 a.m. to 4 p.m.; Visa, Amex, Euro.*

Second choice, but not bad. All types of Levi's clothes for half price, from underwear to overalls. For 501 fans in search of a bargain.

Kleidermarkt Colours
I 9 *Bergmannstrasse 102 (Kreuzberg); Mehringdamm subway station;*

4. PRENZLAUER BERG
Schönhauser Allee
The mixture of students, punks, hipsters, fashionable characters, and people from the neighborhood has created a pleasant atmosphere, where there is no shortage of bars or good secondhand stores.

5. STEGLITZ
Schlossstrasse
A favorite among middle-class shoppers, with big department stores like Karstadt and Wertheim, along with the Galleria, a passage lined with small, interesting shops. The people of Steglitz have no reason to leave their own neighborhood.

6. KREUZBERG
Bergmannstrasse/ Marheinekeplatz
Secondhand stores, antique stores, and junk shops along with Turkish vegetable sellers and bookstores that cater to specific tastes, like the mystery bookshop Hammett.

7. NEUKÖLLN
Karl-Marx-Strasse
If you want to go out shopping in your tennis socks, Karl-Marx-Strasse is a good place for it. It is the longest shopping street in Berlin, and also one of the most affordable. Department stores like Hertie and C&A dominate. There are döner kebab stands everywhere, as well as Turkish grocery stores, bakeries, and obscure import-export shops.

8. SCHEUNENVIERTEL AND SPANDAUER VORSTADT
The new "in" quarter, especially around the restored business district: the Hackesche Höfe is the center of the new Berlin. Many shops have taken up residence, along with theaters, cinemas, restaurants, cafés, and galleries.

PHOTOS: Jörg Lehmann (2)

A renaissance of past epochs: Falbala

Tel. 694 33 48; Monday through Wednesday 11 a.m. to 7 p.m., Thursday, Friday 11 a.m. to 8 p.m., Saturday 10 a.m. to 4 p.m.; no credit cards.

'70s and '80s vintage clothing, mostly from the United States.

Falbala

K 4 Knaackstrasse 43 (Prenzlauer Berg); Eberswalder Strasse subway station; Tel. 44 05 10 82; Monday through Friday 1 p.m. to 6 p.m., Saturday 12 noon through 2 p.m.; Euro, Visa, Amex.

Fashions from 1880 to 1980. Fabulous cocktail clothes for fabulous women with fabulous amounts of money.

Garage

G 7 Ahornstrasse 2 (Schöneberg); Nollendorfplatz subway station; Tel. 211 27 60; Monday through Wednesday 11 a.m. to 7 p.m., Thursday, Friday 11 a.m. to 8 p.m., Saturday 10 a.m. to 4 p.m.; no credit cards.

Clothes for sale by the kilo. Price: DM 25.95. An enormous selection for a young, hip crowd.

Macy's

D 7 Mommsenstrasse 2 (Charlottenburg); Uhlandstrasse subway station; Tel. 881 13 63; Monday through Friday 11 a.m. to 6:30 p.m., Saturday 11 a.m. to 4 p.m.; all credit cards.

Secondhand designer fashions by Armani, Jil Sander, Versace, and Prada.

Megastores

Potsdamer Platz Arkaden

H 7 Potsdamer Platz (Mitte); Potsdamer Platz subway station; every day 10 a.m. to 8 p.m.

A glassed-in shopping mall on three floors. About 140 shops, cafés, and restaurants welcome visitors.

Kulturkaufhaus Dussmann

I 7 Friedrichstrasse 90 (Mitte); Friedrichstrasse subway station; Tel. 20 25 20 59; Monday through Saturday 10 a.m. to 10 p.m.; Visa, Euro, Amex.

A spacious, comfortable store with books, CDs, videos, and more.

Department Store 206

I 6 Friedrichstrasse 71 (Mitte); Französische Strasse subway station; Tel. 20 94 62 76; Monday through Friday 10 a.m. to 8 p.m., Saturday 10 a.m. to 4 p.m.; all credit cards.

A luxury shopping complex featuring DKNY, Etro, Strenesse, Gabriele Strehle, Gucci, B54, a store for eyeglasses,

and the furniture store Out of Asia.

Department stores

KaDeWe

F 7 Tauentzienstrasse 21-24 (Charlottenburg); Wittenbergplatz subway station; Tel. 212 10; Monday through Friday 9:30 a.m. to 8 p.m., Saturday 9 a.m. to 4 p.m.; all credit cards.

Germany's biggest department store. The highlight is the gourmet food section, especially the Lenôtre confection area.

Galeries Lafayette

I 7 Friedrichstrasse – Quartier 206 (Mitte); Französische Strasse subway station; Tel. 20 94 80; Monday through Friday 9:30 a.m. to 8 p.m., Saturday 10 a.m. to 4 p.m.; all credit cards.

All the high-priced brands for clothing and accessories. Already a legend.

Jewelry

Schauder & Jundef

E 8 Fasanenstrasse 73 (Charlottenburg); Kufürstendamm subway station; Tel. 882 13 84; Monday through Friday 10:30 a.m. to 4 p.m., Saturday 10 a.m. to 4 p.m.; Amex, Visa, Master, Euro.

The only place where you'll find the Master Banker, a watch that shows the time in three different parts of the world.

Bulgari
E 8 *Fasanenstrasse 70
(Charlottenburg); Uhland-
strasse subway station;
Tel. 885 79 20; Monday
through Friday 10 a.m. to
7 p.m., Saturday 10 a.m. to
4 p.m.; Visa, Amex,
Master, Euro, Diners.*
Opulent Italian shop
with a beautiful marble
façade. Exclusively
Bulgari.

Cartier
E 7 *Fasanenstrasse 28
(Charlottenburg); Uhland-
strasse subway station;
Tel. 886 70 60; Monday
through Friday 10 a.m. to
7 p.m., Saturday 10 a.m. to
4 p.m.; Amex, Visa, Mas-
ter, Euro.*
We recommend the
diamond brooch at DM
26,200. (For an additio-
nal DM 17,450 you can
also get matching ear-
rings.)

Bizarre

Ave Maria &
Devotionalien
G 7 *Potsdamer Strasse 75
(Tiergarten); Kurfürsten-
strasse subway station;
Tel. 262 12 11; Monday
through Friday 12 noon to
7 p.m., Saturday 12 noon
to 3 p.m.; no credit cards.*
Everything for your
home altar: candles,
pictures of saints, rosa-

*Altar offerings: Ave
Maria Devotionalien*

ries, and even a plaster
Mother Theresa.

Kaufhaus Schrill
D 7 *Bleibtreustrasse 46
(Charlottenburg); Savi-
gnyplatz S-Bahn station;
Tel. 882 40 48; Monday
through Friday 11 a.m. to
7 p.m., Saturday 10 a.m. to
4 p.m.; Euro, Amex, Visa.*
The best place for fake
jewelry, feather boas,
ties, cufflinks, headgear,
and much more. Where
film costume designers
come to shop.

Hautnah Eccentric
Fashion
E 8 *Uhlandstrasse 170
(Charlottenburg); Uhland-
strasse subway station;
Tel. 882 34 34; Monday
through Friday 12 noon to
8 p.m., Saturday 10 a.m. to
4 p.m.; no credit cards.*
Two floors of rubber,
latex, and leather. A
favorite among the S&M
crowd.

Auctions

Villa Griesebach
E 8 *Fasanenstrasse 25
(Charlottenburg); Uhland-
strasse subway station;
Tel. 885 91 50; Monday
through Friday 10 a.m. to
6:30 p.m.; no credit cards.*
Germany's biggest
auction house for art-
works from the nine-
teenth and twentieth
centuries.

Kunstauktionshaus
Prinz-Dunst
D 7 *Schlüterstrasse 16
(Charlottenburg), Savi-
gnyplatz S-Bahn station;
Tel. 312 5147; Monday
through Friday 10 a.m. to
1 p.m. and 2 p.m. to 6*

*For the wild at heart:
Kaufhaus Schrill*

*p.m., Saturday 10 a.m. to 1
p.m.; no credit cards.*
Auctions of glass, porce-
lain, silver, paintings,
sculptures, and Thai
Buddhas.

Street markets &
Shopping halls

Marheinekehalle
I 9 *Marheinekeplatz 15
(Kreuzberg); Gneisenau-
strasse subway station;
Monday through Friday
7:30 a.m. to 6 p.m., Saturday 7:30 a.m. to 2 p.m.*
Fruit and vegetable
stands side by side with
tailors, hairdressers, and
travel agents. Like a trip
back in time.

Winterfeldtmarkt
G 8 *Winterfeldtplatz
(Schöneberg) Nollendorf-
platz subway station;
Wednesday, Saturday 8
a.m. to 1 p.m.*
The best of Berlin's
outdoor markets. An
enormous range of
culinary offerings, from
Canadian blueberry
muffins to Arabic humus.

Turkish Market on
Maybachufer
K 8 *Maybachufer,
between Kottbusser Brücke
and Schinkestrasse
(Neukölln); subway
station Kottbusser Damm
and Tor; Friday, Tuesday
12 noon to 6:30 p.m.*

PHOTOS: Jörg Lehmann (3)

Kreuzberg's Turkish families come here to shop—a sign of quality.

Books

Ufo–Phantastische Buchhandlung (Fantasy Bookshop)

I 9 *Bergmannstrasse 25 (Kreuzberg); Gneisenaustrasse subway station; Tel. 69 50 51 17; Monday through Friday 10 a.m. to 8 pm., Saturday 9 a.m. to 4 p.m.; Visa.*

A temple for *Star Trek* and *Star Wars* fans. Everything about sci-fi, horror, and fantasy. Collectors can find original editions from the U.S.

Bücherbogen

E 7 *Am Stadtbahnbogen 593 (Charlottenburg); Savignyplatz S-Bahn station; Tel. 312 19 32; Monday through Friday 10 a.m. to 8 p.m., Saturday 10 a.m. to 4 p.m.; Euro, Visa, Master.*

Specialty bookshop for fashion, design, art, architecture, photography, and film.

Prinz Eisenherz

D 7 *Bleibtreustrasse 52 (Charlottenburg); Savignyplatz subway station; Tel. 313 99 36; Monday through Friday 10 a.m. to 7 p.m., Saturday 10 a.m. to 4 p.m.; Visa, Euro.*

Titles for gays. This is considered by some to be the best-arranged specialty bookshop in the world.

Grober Unfug

I 8 *Zossener Strasse 32-33 (Kreuzberg); Gneisenaustrasse subway station; Tel. 69 40 14 92; Monday* through Friday 11 a.m. to 7 p.m., Saturday 11 a.m. to 4 p.m.; Euro, Visa, Amex.

Berlin's best store for comic books. Also includes a gallery.

Records & CDs

Mr Dead & Mrs Free

G 8 *Bülowstrasse 5 (Schöneberg); Nollendorfplatz subway station; Tel. 215 14 49; Monday through Wednesday 11 a.m. to 7 p.m., Thursday, Friday 11 a.m. to 8 p.m., Saturday 11 a.m. to 4 p.m.; no credit cards.*

A shop for independent labels and imports which has become an institution.

Unter den Gleisen

I 5 *Friedrichstrasse 128 (Mitte); Oranienburger Tor subway station; Tel. 285 91 44; Monday through Friday 10 a.m. to 8 p.m., Saturday 10 a.m. to 4 p.m.; no credit cards.*

Jazz, Latin, hip-hop, house, and GDR labels, also secondhand. Lots of vinyl and therefore a hot address for DJs.

Gelbe Musik

E 8 *Schaperstrasse 11 (Wilmersdorf); Spichernstrasse subway station; Tel. 211 39 62; Tuesday through Friday 1 p.m. to 6 p.m., Saturday 11 a.m. to 2 p.m.; Euro, Visa, Amex.*

A treasure trove for fans of the avant. Helpful employees dig up anything ever put on vinyl or CD.

Esoteric

Feng Shui – der Laden

F 8 *Welser Strasse 10 (Schöneberg) Viktoria-* Luise-Platz subway station; Tel. 211 17 71; Monday, Wednesday, Friday 11 a.m. to 6:30 p.m.; Thursday 11 a.m. to 8 p.m., Saturday 10 a.m. to 3 p.m.; no credit cards.

Everything for living in harmony, according to the Chinese art.

Kansal

I 8 *Gneisenaustrasse 114 (Kreuzberg); Gneisenaustrasse subway station; Tel. 692 23 00; Monday through Friday 11 a.m. to 6 p.m., Saturday 10 a.m. to 2 p.m.; no credit cards.*

Ayurvedic products of all kinds, from Indian flea seeds to nose jewelry.

Interior decoration

Karthago

D 7 *Pestalozzistrasse 105 (Charlottenburg); Savignyplatz S-Bahn station; Tel. 80 60 48 03; Monday, Wednesday, Friday 10 a.m. to 7 p.m., Thursday 10 a.m. to 4 p.m., Saturday 10 a.m. to 4 p.m.; no credit cards.*

Treasures from Egypt, Syria, and Jordan sheltered beneath a desert tent in Charlottenburg.

Find the proper arrangements: Feng Shui

*Handle with care:
art + industry*

Habitare

D 7 *Savignyplatz 7-8
(Charlottenburg); Savi-
gnyplatz station; Tel. 31
86 47 11; Monday
through Friday 10 a.m. to
8 p.m., Saturday 10 a.m. to
4 p.m.; no credit cards.*
A large selection of
interesting furniture at
affordable prices. Friendly
service and fast deliveries.

Antiques

art + industry

D 7 *Bleibtreustrasse 40
(Charlottenburg) Savigny-
platz S-Bahn station; Tel.
883 49 46; Monday
through Friday 2 p.m. to
6:30 p.m., Saturday 11 a.m.
to 4 p.m.; no credit cards.*
Features handmade art
objects and industrial
design. Beautiful steel
furniture from the '30s
and old timepieces.

Das alte Bureau

G 8 *Goltzstrasse 6
(Schöneberg); Nollendorf-
platz subway station; Tel.
216 59 50; Monday
through Friday 3 p.m. to
6:30 p.m., Saturday 11 a.m.
to 3 p.m.; no credit cards.*
Fantastic office
furniture, from the 19th
century to the 1920s.

China antik

I 5 *Auguststrasse 28
(Mitte); Oranienburger
Strasse S-Bahn station;
Tel. 28 38 44 05; Tuesday*

through Friday 3 p.m. to 7
p.m., Saturday 12 noon to
4 p.m.; Amex, Visa, Euro.
Chinese antiques, re-
stored in workshops in
their home country.

Flea markets

Antik- und Trödel-
markt (Antique and
Junk Market)

L 7 *Hauptbahnhof
(Friedrichshain); Haupt-
bahnhof S-Bahn station;
Tel. 29 00 20 10; Saturday
9 a.m. to 3 p.m., Sunday
10 a.m. to 5 p.m.*
Collectors items from
the '50s and '60s, with a
large selection of old
newspapers.

Kunstmarkt

E 6 *Strasse des 17. Juni;
Tiergarten S-Bahn station;
Tel. 26 55 00 96; Saturday,
Sunday 8 a.m to 4 p.m.*
The ultimate place to
find furniture and
lamps. A good selection
of art deco objects.

Flohmarkt am
Arkonaplatz
Fleamarket

J 4 *Arkonaplatz (Pankow);
Bernauer Strasse subway
station; Tel. 93 79 87 55;
Sunday 10 a.m. to 4 p.m.*
Enjoyable neighborhood
atmosphere in a former
blue-collar district. Lots
of items from people's
homes, with a good
selection of records and
books.

Gifts

Whiskey & Cigars

J 5 *Sophienstrasse 23
(Mitte); Hackescher*

Markt S-Bahn station; Tel.
282 03 76; Tuesday
through Friday 12 noon to
7 p.m., Saturday 11 a.m. to
4 p.m.; no credit cards.*
Big selection of Scotch and
bourbon and a gigantic
selection of cigars.

Küchenladen

E 7 *Knesebeckstrasse 26
(Charlottenburg); Savi-
gnyplatz S-Bahn station;
Tel. 881 39 08; Monday
through Friday 10 a.m. to
7 p.m., Saturday 10 a.m. to
4 p.m.; Euro, Visa.*
Where serious cooks
come to shop.
Everything a serious
culinary artist requires,
from a device for making
melon balls to the very
latest in high-tech pots.

Ararat

I 9 *Bergmannstrasse 99a
(Kreuzberg); Gneisenau-
strasse S-Bahn station;
Tel. 693 50 80; Monday
through Friday 10 a.m. to
8 p.m., Saturday 10 a.m. to
4 p.m.; Visa.*
Paradise for postal
enthusiasts. Tons of
postcards, and a lot of
unusual writing
materials.

*High proof:
Whiskey & Cigars*

beauty

Aveda

E 7 *Kurfürstendamm 29 (Charlottenburg); Kurfürstendamm subway station; Tel. 88 55 27 57; Monday through Friday 10 a.m. to 8 p.m., Saturday 9 a.m. to 4 p.m.; Amex, Euro, Visa.*

Skin and haircare products, all made from plants. Incredibly relaxing aromatherapy.

KaDeWe

F 7 *Tauentzienstrasse 21-24 (Charlottenburg); Wittenbergplatz subway station; Tel. 212 10; Monday through Friday 9:30 a.m. to 8 p.m., Saturday 9 a.m. to 4 p.m.; Amex, Diners, Euro.*

Berlin's consumer temple has counters by Chanel, Helena Rubinstein, Shiseido, Clinique, Brown, and M.A.C.

Belladonna

I 9 *Bergmannstrasse 101 (Kreuzberg); Gneisenaustrasse subway station; Tel. 694 37 31; Monday through Friday 10 a.m. to 7 p.m., Saturday 10 a.m. to 4 p.m.; Visa, Euro, Amex.*

Ethereal oils, fragrant shampoos and aromatic balsam. If you are receiving a cosmetic treatment you can try all the products.

DK Cosmetics

D 7 *Kurfürstendamm 56 (Charlottenburg); Savignyplatz S-Bahn station; Tel. 32 79 01 23; Monday through Wednesday 10 a.m. to 7 p.m., Thursday, Friday 10 a.m. to 8 p.m., Saturday 10 a.m. to 4 p.m.; Amex, Diner, Euro, Visa.*

Luxury products for people with avant-garde tastes. DK Cosmetics also has a nail bar.

Upscale in Mitte: Department Store Quartier 206

Department Store Quartier 206

I 6 *Friedrichstrasse 71 (Mitte); Französische Strasse subway station; Tel. 20 94 68 00; Monday through Friday 10 a.m. to 8 p.m., Saturday 10 a.m. to 4 p.m.; Amex, Diners, Euro, Visa.*

In the World of Beauty you will find practically every fragrance on earth.

Udo Walz

E 7 *Kempinski Plaza, Uhlandstrasse 181 (Charlottenburg); Savignyplatz S-Bahn station; Tel. 826 61 08; Tuesday through Friday 9:30 a.m. to 6:30 p.m., Saturday 9:30 a.m. to 1:30 p.m.; Amex, Visa, Master, Euro.*

Udo Walz has had some famous customers, including Herbert von Karajan, Leonard Bernstein, Catherine Deneuve, and Demi Moore.

Toni & Guy

C 7 *Kaiser-Friedrich-Strasse 1a; Charlottenburg S-Bahn station; Tel. 341 85 45; Monday 1 p.m. to 6:30 p.m., Tuesday through Friday 9 a.m. to 8 p.m., Saturday 9 a.m. to 2 p.m.; Amex, Visa, Master, Euro.*

Toni & Guy are said to have a finely-attuned sense of the latest trends. Haircuts from DM 75.

Die Besten vom anderen Ufer

L 8 *Ohlauer Strasse 40 (Kreuzberg); Görlitzer Bahnhof subway station; Tel. 612 73 19; Monday through Friday 10 a.m. to 8 p.m., Saturday 10 a.m. to 1 p.m.; no credit cards.*

A wide range of customers: punks, artists, media types, and the occasional grandmother from the neighborhood. Haircuts from DM 52.

Haarem

G 8 *Winterfeldtstrasse 33 (Schöneberg); Nollendorfplatz subway station; Tel. 216 37 25; Tuesday through Friday 10 a.m. to 7 p.m., Saturday 10 a.m. to 3 p.m.; no credit cards.*

Hot haircuts for the cool crowd. Women DM 75, men DM 45.

Silvana Sonsalla Cosmetic

G 7 *Grand Hotel Esplanade, Lützowufer 15 (Tiergarten); Nollendorfplatz subway station; Tel. 25 47 82 52; Monday through Friday 9 a.m. to 8 p.m.; Amex, Visa, Euro, Master .*

This modern studio easily captivates one with its elegant atmosphere and its large selection of different body care treatments.

Cabinebleue

H 7 *Grand Hyatt, Marlene-Dietrich-Platz 2 (Tiergarten); Potsdamer Platz subway and S-Bahn station; Tel. 25 53 12 34; daily 6:30 a.m. to 12 p.m.; Amex, Visa, Euro, Master, Diners.*

Offers a wide range of treatments: body massage, foot reflexology, shiatsu head massage, lomi-lomi, tui-na, reiki, and massage with aromatic oils.

Shiseido Beauty Gallery

D 7 *Bleibtreustrasse 32 (Charlottenburg); Uhlandstrasse subway station; Tel. 88 67 98 40; Monday through Friday 10 a.m. to 7 p.m., Saturday 10 a.m. to 4 p.m.; no credit cards.*

This is the place to try all the different products by the Japanese cosmetic manufacturer. Unfortunately, none of them are for sale here, because the Gallery is supposed to be a kind of cosmetics communications center.

Biotherm Aveda Day Spa

E 7 *Kurfürstendamm 29 (Charlottenburg); Uhlandstrasse subway station; Tel. 88 55 27 57; Monday through Friday 10 a.m. to 8 p.m., Saturday 10 a.m. to 4 p.m.; Amex, Visa, Master, Euro.*

Offers Aveda massages, facials, manicures, and pedicures. Best to make a reservation in advance.

Solariums

Jopp Sun

D 7 *Leibnizstrasse 61 (Charlottenburg); Adenauerplatz subway station; Tel. 793 37 52; Monday through Friday 7 a.m. to 10 p.m., Saturday, Sunday 10 a.m. to 8 p.m.; no credit cards.*

Tanning from DM 5 with air-conditioned Ergoline beds.

Siesta

L 7 *Pücklerstrasse 18 (Kreuzberg); Görlitzer Bahnhof subway station; Tel. 61 28 02 30; Monday through Friday 10 a.m. to 9 p.m., Saturday 10 a.m. to 6 p.m., Sunday 1 p.m. to 6 p.m.; no credit cards.*

A good studio with excellent staff. Power tanning beds in top condition.

Tattoo/Piercing

Tatau Obscure

I 9 *Solmsstrasse 35 (Kreuzberg); Gneisenaustrasse subway station; Tel. 69 44 42 88; Tuesday through Friday 1 p.m. to 7 p.m., Saturday 1 p.m. to 5 p.m.; no credit cards.*

Henna paintings and tattoos. The shop also has art objects, books, and pictures, which you can buy or just use for inspiration.

Body Temple

G 8 *Nollendorfstrasse 24 (Schöneberg); Nollendorfplatz subway station; Tel. 217 56 282; Monday through Friday 1 p.m. to 8 p.m., Saturday 11 a.m. to 3 p.m.; Euro, Visa, Amex.*

Everything from the world of body art: tattoos, piercing, natural cosmetics, permanent epilation, and tattoo removal.

Gerhard Meir

Two years ago the star hairdresser opened a salon in Berlin.

MAX CITY GUIDE: Can you recognize a woman from Berlin by her haircut?
GERHARD MEIR: Yes. Women from Berlin have an insanely good combination of styles: very avant-garde and at the same time "shabby chic." Perfect and distinctly different.
Q: You have created Berlin haircuts. What do they look like?
A: A mixture of extravagance and an anti-haircut: push the hair upwards and allow a few strands to fall down. Or smooth hair, with a single lock hanging down in front of the face.

Le Coup

I 6 *in the Hotel Adlon, Unter den Linden 77 (Mitte); Unter den Linden S-Bahn station; Tel.: 22 66 77 0; Monday through Friday 9 a.m. to 6:30 p.m., Saturday 9 a.m. to 2 p.m.*

PHOTOS: Jorg Lehmann (2), Dejan (3)

Angela Marquardt, 27

Her constituency is in Ludwigslust. Although she was the acting PDS (Party of Democratic Socialism) chairwoman from 1995 to 1997, she did not have a seat in the Bundestag until 1998.

Dirk Niebel, 36

Liberal and proud of it. A member of the FDP (Free Democratic Party), Niebel's whole life is dedicated to politics. He ran in Heidelberg and made it into the Bundestag on his first try, no mean feat for a small party Rep.

Cem Özdemir, 33

The first prominent politician in Germany with a Turkish background. Even though he doesn't like to hear it, Özdemir has good chances of becoming the first government minister from an immigrant family.

Katherina Reiche, 25

Black is beautiful. The CDU (Christian Democratic Party) used to run with this slogan, and Katherine Reiche, from Luckenwalde bei Potsdam, must have taken it to heart. Many people in the Brandenburg CDU think she has a glowing future.

Carsten Schneider, 23

He is the youngest member of parliament. But there is more to the story: his education was as a bank clerk, and if he had not gone into politics, he would now be sharing the fate of many people his age: he wouldn't have a job.

Where and pe

nightlife

The relocation of the capital to Berlin is opening new worlds for representatives of the people. In the future they will meet voters in the crowded bars and pubs in Mitte. We sent five young parliamentarians out for a night on the town.

Text by Dirk Krömer,
Photos by Manuel Krug

politics
ople meet

t he water pipe divides people into two camps. At the Jewish restaurant Oren, it is customary to smoke a few puffs after a good meal. It's completely harmless: instead of tobacco or anything stronger, the pipe glows with a kind of fruit briquette, and the sweet steam is inhaled through a hose with a straw on the end. But for up-and-coming young CDU politico Katherina Reiche, this public inhaling is a little too much. "I don't want anything to do with drugs," says the representative. Dirk Niebel of the FDP also refuses to indulge: "I recently quit smoking, so I don't want to try this."

The people from left-leaning parties have no problem with the pipe. Angela Marquardt (PDS) and

Carsten Schneider (SPD) form a red-red smoking coalition. And Cem Özdemir lives up to the cliché about how all members of the Green Party know about drugs: he puffs away like a chimney and gives his expert opinion: "Mild, very mild, with one caveat: it seems to be missing something."

Everyone is curious. Five members of parliament from the five different factions go on a pub crawl in a neighborhood that will soon be their home base: Berlin Mitte, the seat of the German Bundestag beginning in the summer of 1999. All of them are curious about the city's nightlife, except for Angela Marquardt, who came to Berlin to study and has been living in Prenzlauer Berg for more than three years. Although her party is accused of being a shelter for lost souls of German reunification, she is a winner through and through. This

Some 'Mitte hotspots' can accomodate only so many more drunken pols.

summer, politics are coming to her, and she doesn't have to go to Bonn anymore for parliamentary sessions. Katherine Reiche already knows the neighborhood. "In the days of East Germany, class trips to Berlin were compulsory," she recalls. (It doesn't sound like it was a good experience.) She is clearly delighted that the seat of government is moving close to her home in Luckenwalde, which is about fifty kilometers south of Berlin. But she's definitely no country bumpkin, and she loves a rocking night out— she is the one who suggests going to Oren. Unfortunately, the stress of running the state does not leave her a lot of time for the more agreeable aspects of political life.

Dirk Niebel nods and orders a Hefeweizen. He could tell you many stories about tough times in the life of a politician. His wife and his two children are in Heidelberg—often left by themselves. When the government was still in Bonn, he could usually make it home, even if it was late. "I didn't have an apartment there, so I used to drive home every night," he says. But now he has started looking for a place in Berlin. "I'm not even concerned about what part of the city it's in, I just don't want to live in some bunker for MPs."

The idea of living with other MPs doesn't appeal to Carsten Schneider, either. The twenty-three-year-old thinks it's important to spend time with people not in the same profession as he is. In Bonn it's hard to meet anyone who's *not* connected to politics, and for that reason alone he's happy to be moving. (Also he thinks the bars in Berlin are much better). Carsten is from Erfurt, and the move will bring him closer to his constituency, his family, and his old friends who helped him fight his way up through the party ranks.

Fears

Cem Özdemir is very happy when he thinks about the new Berlin Republic. But he also has some reasons to be afraid. Cem is considered one of the brightest and most articulate members of the Green Party, and because he has Turkish parents and a German passport, his every word is held under a microscope whenever a political issue arises involving Turks or Kurds. He doesn't mince words in such situations, but talks frankly about human rights violations by the Turkish government and the fanatic nationalism of the Kurds. Radical Turks and Kurds consider him their enemy—and there are more representatives of both groups in Berlin than in any other city.

He is protected by bodyguards, but the situation does not bother him too much—he even sees a certain humor in it. And his colleague Dirk Niebel can scarcely conceal his enthusiasm: "They pick you up in the morning and then bring you home again at night? Great! I'd love it!"

nightlife

Bars

Bar am Lützowplatz
G 8 *Lützowplatz 7 (Tiergarten); Kurfürstenstrasse subway station; Tel. 262 68 07; daily 5 p.m. to 4 a.m.; Amex, Euro, Visa.*

The longest bar in Berlin. A popular hangout for rich and beautiful people. Happy hour until 9 p.m.

Engelspalast im Schwarzenraben
J 5 *Neue Schönhauser Strasse 13 (Mitte); Hackescher Markt S-Bahn station; Tel. 28 39 16 98; daily 10 a.m. to 4 a.m.; Amex, Diners, Euro, Visa.*

The Engelpalast is located deep in the catacombs of the Schwarzenraben. A meeting place for hipsters from all around the city.

Planet Hollywood
I 5 *Friedrichstrasse 68 (Mitte); Friedrichstrasse subway station; Tel. 20 94 58 00; Sunday through Thursday 11:30 a.m. to 1 a.m.; Amex, Euro, Visa.*

Apple strudel made according to a recipe from Arnold Schwarzenegger's mother. Arnie, Sylvester Stallone, and Bruce Willis are the owners.

"Sex on the beach" at Lützowplatz?

Happy hour from 11 p.m. to 1 a.m.

Hudson Bar
G 9 *Elssholzstrasse 10 (Schöneberg); Eisenacher Strasse subway station; Tel. 216 16 02; Friday, Saturday 9 p.m. to 3 a.m.; Amex, Euro, Visa.*

The biggest, strongest drinks in Berlin. Also has an excellent selection of whiskeys and cognacs.

NN-Train
G 9 *In the Kleistpark (Schöneberg); Kleistpark subway station; Tel. 787 50 33; opens daily at 5 p.m.; no credit cards.*

A remodeled S-Bahn car full of sociable women and well-dressed bank clerks. The terrace is a big attraction in the summer.

Würgeengel
K 8 *Dresdener Strasse 122 (Kreuzberg); Kottbusser Tor subway station; Tel. 615 55 60; opens daily at 7 p.m.; Euro.*

Although the bar seems a little too chic for this part of the city, it is surprisingly popular among people in the neighborhood. The gold roof and the red walls create a pleasant atmosphere.

Live Music

Arena/Glashaus
Treptow Eichenstrasse 4; Treptower Park S-Bahn station; Tel. 533 73 33; Fridays and Saturdays from 11 p.m.; no credit cards.

Formerly a maintenance hall for trams, this is now a popular place for concerts and other events, including a Marlboro Sunday brunch, a fashion show

No tickets necessary: NN-Train

for secondhand clothes, and an appearance by the band Boyzone.

Tempodrom
L 7 *Hauptbahnhof/ Strasse der Pariser Kommune; Tel. 61 28 42 35; open from May 21; no credit cards.*

A legendary venue, located under a big tent. Now fans have to walk a

Jazz singer in Jackson pose

few streets further than they used to, because the former chancellor felt threatened by the subculture. After leaving its current location near the Hauptbahnhof sometime in the year 2001, Tempodrom will finally have a fixed address near Anhalter Bahnhof.

Junction Bar
I 9 *Gneisenaustrasse 18 (Kreuzberg); Gneisenaustrasse subway station; Tel. 694 66 02; daily from 8 p.m.; no credit cards.*

Live shows in the front, and DJs in the back, with a different type of music depending on what day of the week it is. Offers the full range of current trends: hip-hop, rock, jazz. A cult phenomenon.

Schlot
J 4 *Kastanienallee 29 (Prenzlauer Berg); Eberswalder Strasse subway station; Tel. 448 21 60; daily from 7:30 p.m.; no credit cards.*

A small, smoky club in Prenzlauer Berg. A favorite meeting place among the local jazz scene. The stage also serves as a forum for students from the Jazz & Rock School, to which the club is connected.

Miles
L 4 *Greifswalder Strasse 212-213 (Prenzlauer Berg); Huflandstrasse tram stop; Tel. 44 00 81 40; Tuesday through Saturday 8 p.m. to 3 a.m.; no credit cards.*

The successor to the legendary Franz Club features jazz, blues, and soul. Jam sessions are held on Wednesdays. Low-priced drinks are another attraction.

Tränenpalast
I 6 *In the Reichstagsufer 17 (Mitte);*

Friedrichstrasse S-Bahn station; Tel. 20 61 00 11; no credit cards.

A fantastic club on a historic street. A wide range of events: variety theater, fashion shows, concerts, and live broadcasts of sporting events.

Kalkscheune
I 5 *Johannisstrasse 2 (Mitte); Oranienburgerstrasse subway station; Tel. 28 39 00 65; no credit cards.*

Cabaret and tango nights, parties and punk concerts. The courtyard is open in the summer.

Kulturbrauerei
K 4 *Knaackstrasse 97; (Prenzlauer Berg); Eberswalder Strasse subway station; Tel. 441 92 69; no credit cards.*

All kinds of different events on what used to be the grounds of the Schultheiss brewery. The Ostalgie-Partys (retro nights) are a legend. Coming soon: a multiplex cinema.

Pfefferberg/Sub-ground
K 4 *Schönhauser Allee 176 (Prenzlauer Berg); Senefelder Platz subway station; Tel. 449 65 34; club: Thursday through Saturday from 11 p.m.; no credit cards.*

Well-established as a scene-club and a venue for reggae and hip-hop events. With a big beer garden for hanging out on warm summer nights.

Not what it used to be: Tacheles.

Tacheles
I 5 *Oranienburger Strasse 54-56 (Mitte); Oranienburger Tor subway station; Tel. 282 61 85; daily from 12 noon (café), 7 p.m. (cinema), Monday through Friday 2 p.m. to 11 p.m. (gallery); no credit cards.*
Tacheles has lost a lot of its former charm. A popular destination for tourists with anarchist tendencies. Features rock, alternative, and live techno.

Cabaret

Wühlmäuse
F 8 *Nürnberger Strasse 33 (Wilmersdorf); Augsburger Strasse subway station; Tel. 213 70 47; Tickets on sale: Tuesday through Saturday 10 a.m. to 8 p.m.; Euro, Visa.*
Legendary Berlin cabaret. This is also where the owner, Didi Hallervorden, records his TV show *Spott-Light*. A good place to see the most famous names in German comedy.

Die Distel
I 5 *Friedrichstrasse 101 (Mitte); Friedrichstrasse subway and S-Bahn station; Tel. 204 47 04; Tickets on sale: Monday through Friday 12 a.m. to 6 p.m.; no credit cards.*

Founded in 1953, this was the only East German political cabaret that deserved to be taken seriously. Still a favorite among both East and West Berliners.

La Vie en Rose
I 9 *Güntzelstrasse 117; Platz der Luftbrücke subway station; Tel. 69 51 30 00; Visa.*
Erotic and exotic; artistry, magic, comedy, and travesty presented by the Revue-Theater at Tempelhof Airport. If you sit close to the action, you might be pulled onto the stage by the snake charmer or a magician.

Lounges

Castros Zigarren Lounge
E 8 *Pfalzburger Strasse 72a (Wilmersdorf); Uhlandstrasse subway station; Tel. 882 18 08; daily 5 p.m. to 1 a.m.; Euro, Visa.; Creole, Caribbean, and Italian cuisine. Put a nice end to your day with tapas, wine, and a Cuban cigar.*

Cibo Matto
J 5 *Rosenthaler Strasse 44 (Mitte); Weinmeisterstrasse subway station; Tel. 28 38 51 70; all credit cards.*
A new hipster meeting point in Mitte. Modern wood, steel, and glass interior. Seats by the window offer a view of the Hackesche Höfe—but they're hard to come by.

Akba Lounge
K 4 *Sredzkistrasse 64 (Prenzlauer Berg); Senefelder Platz subway station; Tel. 441 14 63; no credit cards.*
A trendy lounge, with music ranging from acid jazz to soul to pop. Chic young crowd.

Kahuna Lounge
J 9 *Körtestrasse 5 (Kreuzberg); Südstern subway station; Tel. 691 66 26; daily from 6 p.m.; no credit cards.*
Kahuna is the Hawaiian word for "master surfer." The crowd matches the name: cool, hip, unassuming.

Blue Note Bar
F 7/8 *Courbièrestrasse 13 (Schöneberg); Wittenbergplatz subway station; Tel. 218 72 48; Thursday through Saturday from 10 p.m., Sunday from 9 p.m.; Visa.*
Cocktail bar with a relaxed jazz club atmosphere.

La Casa del Habano
E 7 *In the Savoy Hotel, Fasanenstrasse 9-10 (Charlottenburg); Zoo subway station; Tel. 311 03 646; Tuesday through Saturday 11 a.m. to 8 p.m.; Amex, Diners, Euro, Visa.*

The Surgeon General warns... : La Casa del Habano

Wood-paneled walls, yellow leather seats, and dark parquet floors create a serious but friendly atmosphere. Serves cocktails and whiskey with the cigars.

Discos & Clubs

Privat Club
L 8 *Pücklerstrasse 34 (Kreuzberg); Görlitzer Bahnhof subway station; Tel. 611 33 02; Thursday through Saturday from 10 p.m.; no credit cards.*
Underground vault beneath Kreuzberg's Markthalle. Relaxed, almost familiar atmosphere. Varied cultural program features art exhibits, chanson evenings, comedy, and jazz concerts.

House club with taste: WMF

WMF/GayMF
I 5 *Johannisstrasse 19 (Mitte); Friedrichstrasse S-Bahn station; Tel. 262 79 01; Friday through Sunday from 11 p.m.; no credit cards.*
A legend of the Berlin house club scene, located in the former

guest house of the Council of Ministers in East Berlin. Gay/MF on Sundays, with house music from the '80s. Entry: DM 15.

Kit Kat Club
L 8 *Glogauer Strasse 2 (Kreuzberg); Görlitzer Bahnhof subway station; Tel. 611 38 33; Wednesday through Sunday from 11 p.m.; no credit cards.*
A bizarre place, and probably not everyone's idea of a good time. Some themes: "Fuck naked sex party only for men," "Sex Trance Bizarre," and "Mystic Rose." Free condoms at the door, and with good reason.

Maria am Ostbahnhof
L 7 *Strasse der Pariser Kommune 8-10 (Friedrichshain); Hauptbahnhof S-Bahn station; Tel. 53 404 82; Wednesday from 8:30 p.m., Thursday through Saturday from 10 p.m.; no credit cards.*

Where's Barbarella? Kurvenstar

The stairwell of a former postal distribution center has become one of Berlin's most successful clubs. Exhibits, performances, concerts, DJ nights. Almost always a rewarding experience.

Icon
J 3 *Cantianstrasse 15 (Prenzlauer Berg); Eberswalder Strasse subway station; Friday through Sunday from 11 p.m.; no credit cards.*
Where drum 'n' bass fans come to meet. Cool atmosphere and a hip crowd, mostly from Prenzlauer Berg and Mitte.

The Hipster: Roter Salon/Grüner Salon
J 5 *Rosa-Luxemburg-Platz, Tel. 24 06 58 07*
Two elegant rooms at the Volksbühne. You can talk for hours in the plush leather armchairs, or dance a tango while listening to cowboy songs. Heavenly.

Insider's tip: Scheinbar Varieté
H 9 *Monumentenstrasse 9, Tel. 784 55 39*
Open stage for anyone who has something to perform. Has been around for more than ten years.

For something a little different: SchwuZ
I 9 *Mehringdamm 61, Tel. 693 70 25*

Willkommen, Bienvenue, Welcome!

By Gayle Tufts

Berlin has a rich tradition of cabaret and variety theater, and there is always something new to see. A short summary for outsiders:

First the classic example:
The Friedrichstadtpalast
I 5 Friedrichstrasse 107, Tel. 23 26 23 26
Productions à la Las Vegas – big, bright and a little over the top. The ballet and orchestra are full of the charm of days past, when world-famous stars like Shirley Bassey used to fire up the audience.

Classic variety theater at
Wintergarten Varieté
G 8 Potsdamer Strasse 96, Tel. 23 08 82 30
This charming venue plays host to the masters of variety: world-famous performers, magicians, and clowns. But be careful: Wintergarten is an expensive pleasure.

The heart of Berlin cabaret beats in the
Bar Jeder Vernunft E 8
Schaperstrasse 24, Tel. 883 15 82
A beautiful art deco circus tent full of mirrors. Excellent food and a constantly changing program, featuring cabaret and comedy. Stars like Georgette Dee and Tim Fischer make regular appearances. One of Germany's most important cultural institutions.

Varieté Kreuzberg style: The
BKA I 9 Mehringdamm 32-34, Tel. 251 01 12
After an interesting ride up in the temperamental elevator, the theater on the sixth floor provides a touch of glamour.

The new generation:
Chamäleon Varieté
J 5 Rosenthaler Strasse 40-41, Tel. 282 71 18 in Hackesche Höfe.
Variety theater performed by young, fresh, unconventional artists.

GAYLE TUFTS has lived in Berlin since 1991 and knows the variety scene inside and out. Her latest CD is called *The Big Show*.

PHOTOS: Jörg Lehmann (3)

Shrill, trashy entertainment in the basement of Berlin's gay center.

SO 36
K 8 *Oranienstrasse 190 (Kreuzberg); Görlitzer Bahnhof subway station; Tel. 61 40 13 06; Monday, Thursday from 11 p.m., Wednesday,* *Friday from 10 p.m., Saturday from 9 p.m., Sunday from 7 p.m.; no credit cards.*
Legendary Kreuzberg club, used to host lots of punk and rock events. These days also features variety theater and dancing. You can feel the breath of history.

Kurvenstar
J 5 Kl. Präsidenten- strasse 4 (Mitte); Hackescher Markt S- Bahn station; Tel. 28 59 97 10; Tuesday through Sunday from 9 p.m.; Friday, Saturday from 9 p.m.; entry: DM 15; Amex, Diners, Euro, Visa.

Offbeat club with '70s style. Bar service in the

Eat with the Stars

Borchardt
I 6 *Französische Strasse 47 (Mitte); Französische Strasse subway station; Tel. 20 38 71 10; daily 11 a.m. to 12 p.m.; Amex, Visa.*
First-class gourmet restaurant with a long list of famous guests, including Karl Lagerfeld and Gerhard Schröder.

Café Einstein
G 8 Kurfürstenstrasse 58 (Tiergarten); U-Bhf. Nollendorfplatz subway station; Tel. 261 50 96; daily 10 a.m. to 2 a.m.; Amex, Visa, Euro.
The atmosphere of a Viennese coffee house. Kaiserschmarren (pancakes sprinkled with pow- dered sugar and raisins) with plums, and Alfred Biolek or Erich Böhme sitting at the next table.

Paris Bar
E 7 Kantstrasse 152 (Charlottenburg); Zoo subway station; Tel. 313 80 52; daily, 12 noon. to 2 a.m.; Amex.
This place is crowded year-round, and not just during the Berlin Film Festival. The food is not the reason why people come here. There are many celebrities to gaze at: Götz George, Iris Berben, Otto Sander, Nadja Auermann, and Claudia Schiffer.

Luther und Wegner
I 6 *Charlottenstrasse 56 (Mitte); Französische Strasse subway station; Tel. 202 95 40; daily 9 a.m. to 2 a.m.; Amex, Euro, Visa.*
Film and theater people meet at the Gendarmenmarkt. Pierce Brosnan, Ben Kingsley, Jil Sander, and Klaus Maria Brandauer have all passed through these doors.

Reinhards
D 8 *Kurfürstendamm 190 (Charlottenburg); Savignyplatz S-Bahn station; Tel. 881 16 21; daily 8 a.m. to 1 a.m.; Amex, Diners.*
A touch of Paris. Berlin's most famous playboy, Rolf Eden, is here practically every day.

Schwarzenraben
J 5 *Neue Schönhauser Strasse 13 (Mitte); Hackescher Markt S-Bahn station; Tel. 28 39 16 98; daily 10 a.m, to 12 p.m.; Amex, Visa, Euro, Diners.*
Featured in many different lifestyle magazines, Schwarzen- raben is where famous people from the worlds of film, advertis- ing, and music come to meet.

Quasimodo:
A jazz legend

front and a dance floor in the back. Music: hip-hop, funk, soul.

Jazz

B-Flat

J 5 *Rosenthaler Strasse 13 (Mitte); Weinmeisterstrasse subway station; Tel. 280 63 49; daily from 8 p.m.; no credit cards.*

Live sessions every day. Modern, cool, experimental. Now features a swing dance evening and a tango night.

Quasimodo

C 7 *Kantstrasse 12 a; (Charlottenburg); Zoo subway station; Tel. 312 80 86; daily from 5 p.m.; no credit cards.*

Legendary Berlin jazz club, located underneath Delphi Kino. The great names make regular appearances.

Pubs

Mutter

F/G 8 *Hohenstaufenstrasse 4 (Schöneberg); Nollendorfplatz subway station; Tel. 216 49 90; daily 8:30 a.m. to 4 a.m.; Euro, Visa.*

Bar with sushi. A favorite meeting place on Saturday evenings after shopping at the Winterfeldtmarkt. Dimly lit, with a quiet atmosphere and food until four in the morning.

Zucca

J 5 *Am Zwirngraben/ Bögen 11-12 (Mitte); Hackescher Markt S-Bahn station; Tel. 24 72 12 12; daily 9 a.m. to 3 a.m.; no credit cards*

This beautiful, generous bar is run by Max Ballauf, an actor on the series *Tatort*. Unfortunately, there is not much else to recommend it.

Ankerklause

K 8 *Kottbusser Brücke/Maybachufer (Kreuzberg); Schönleinstrasse subway station; Tel. 693 56 49; daily from 10 a.m., Monday from 4 p.m.; no credit cards.*

During the day, this is a quiet place, but at night it is crowded and hip. Tip: go on a Thursday, when they open up the tiny dance floor. At some point in evening the staff stops trying to make its way through the masses of people, and drinks are available only at the bar. During the summer the crowds flow out into the street.

Hackbarth's

J 5 *Auguststrasse 49a (Mitte); Weinmeisterstrasse subway station; Tel. 282 77 04; daily 9 a.m. to 3 a.m.; no credit cards.*

Artists, lawyers, architects, and students all meet and mix here in the afternoon and early evening before moving on to one of the many clubs in the area.

Weltrestaurant Markthalle

L 7/8 *Pücklerstrasse 34 (Kreuzberg); Görlitzer Bahnhof subway station; Tel. 617 55 02; daily 9 a.m. to 2 a.m., Sunday from 10 a.m.; Amex, Diners, Euro, Visa.*

An authentic old tavern with the charm of a dusty village pub. Rustic and down to earth, with long wooden tables. An institution.

Keyser Soze

I 5 *Tucholskystrasse 33 (Mitte); Oranienburger Strasse S-Bahn station; Tel. 28 59 94 89; daily 10 a.m. to 3 a.m.; no credit cards.*

Hipster dream: Keyser Soze

An "in" spot in Mitte, despite simple furnishings, indifferent service, and loud music. Nevertheless, a good place to see and be seen.

Obst & Gemüse

I 5 *Oranienburger Strasse 48/ 49 (Mitte); Oranienburger Strasse S-Bahn station; Tel. 282 96 47; daily 9 a.m. to 3 a.m.; no credit cards.*

Places by the windows are hard to come by; if you don't come early you won't have a chance. The advantage: across the street you can see Tacheles and you'll be within reach of the basket with free peanuts.

Golgotha

H 9 *Dudenstrasse 48—64; Platz der Luftbrücke subway station; Tel: 785 24 53; daily 11 a.m. to 6 a.m.*

Legendary Kreuzberg beer garden with seats for 2000 guests on two levels. Still charming despite its enormous size. There is almost always a well-known face somewhere in the crowd.

Luise

Dahlem *Königen-Luise-Strasse 40; Dahlem Dorf subway station; Tel: 832 84 87; daily 10 a.m. to 1 a.m.; no credit cards.*

This beer garden in the middle of the woods is a favorite summer meeting place among students and professors from the Freie Universität in Dahlem. Families from the surrounding area also stop by. Pleasant and relaxed. Shade from the chestnut trees keeps things cool in the summer. Places for 800 guests.

Shaken not stirred: Obst & Gemüse

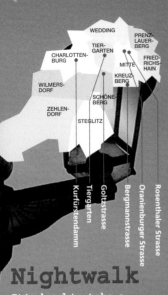

WEDDING
PRENZ-LAUER-BERG
CHARLOTTEN-BURG
TIER-GARTEN
FRIED-RICHS-HAIN
MITTE
WILMERS-DORF
KREUZ-BERG
SCHÖNE-BERG
ZEHLEN-DORF
STEGLITZ

Kurfürstendamm
Tiergarten
Goltzstrasse
Bergmannstrasse
Oranienburger Strasse
Rosenthaler Strasse

Nightwalk

It's hard to take a wrong turn on the streets of Berlin

Kurfürstendamm (Charlottenburg)

E 7 *between Uhlandstrasse and Europa-Center; Kurfürstendamm subway station*

Portrait painters, jugglers, and musicians in front of the Gedächtniskirche. Lots of movie theaters and restaurants. Side streets like Bleibtreustrasse, Knesebeckstrasse, and Grolmanstrasse are known for good cafés, restaurants, and shops.

Rosenthaler Strasse (Mitte)

J 5 *between the Hackescher Markt and Auguststrasse subway stations; Hackescher Markt S-Bahn station*

New cafés and restaurants are springing up here constantly. An influx of tourists and people night-clubbing in Mitte keep things lively until the early hours. Despite the crowds, most of the restaurant and bar courtyards are idyllic.

Oranienburger Strasse (Mitte)

I 5 *between the Oranienburger Tor and Monbijouplatz subway stations; Oranienburger Strasse S-Bahn station*

One bar after another, like Tacheles, grandfather of the alternative scene. Also some alternative restaurants like Oren and Orange, both by the synagogue. Berlin's red-light district is nearby, and so are Kalkscheune and WMF, a legend of the Berlin club scene.

Zoologischer Garten and Strasse des 17. Juni

Zoo subway and S-Bahn station

In the summer Tiergarten is Berlin's number one cruising zone. Follow the railway embankment into Tiergarten. Avoid the Schleusenkrug off to the left. Stop somewhere off to the right, or just start following a group of nice, good-looking men.

Goltzstrasse (Schöneberg)

G 8 *between the Nollendorfplatz and Eisenacher Strasse subway stations*

Walk down Maassenstrasse, toward Goltzstrasse. On the way you will pass lots of cool bars, like Café Berio, Lembach, and Sidney. In Goltzstrasse people from Schöneberg meet in places like Mutter, Café M, Lux or in one of many Indian Imbisses (snack stands).

Bergmannstrasse (Kreuzberg)

I 9 *U-Bahnhof Gneisenaustrasse subway station*

There is a little bit of everything here: snack bars that serve döner kebabs, falafels, or Indian food, along with some terrific restaurants. On Bergmannstrasse we recommend Osteria, Atlantik, and Bergmann 103 are worth trying. Neighboring streets have many small, cosy bars.

PHOTOS: Jörg Lehmann (3)

Folks need food!

If the way to love is through the stomach, the way to sex is via the eyes: Three of Berlin's best chefs tell us their favorite recipes.

Photos by Daniela Eger/Z21

Weltrestaurant Markthalle

Pücklerstrasse 34 (Kreuzberg);
Tel. 617 55 02;
Görlitzer Bahnhof subway station;
Daily 9 a.m. to 3 a.m.;
Amex, Diners, Visa, Euro.

Königsberger Meatballs

Take 300 grams of chopped beef and pork with finely cut anchovies, onions cooked five minutes in butter or oil, and a roll or white bread dipped in milk: form into balls. Season with salt and pepper and cook in salted water with an onion. Mix some of the juices with Grand Marnier. Add capers to the sauce and allow it to cook for ten minutes. Add crème fraîche and lemon juice and garnish with red beets and boiled potatoes.

Sale e Tabacchi

Kochstrasse 18 (Kreuzberg);
Kochstrasse subway station;
Tel. 252 11 55;
daily 12 noon to 12 p.m.;
Amex, Euro, Visa, Diners.

Lobster with Artichokes

4 lobsters up to 300 g each
300 g of butter
50 g bacon
carrots, onions
16 artichoke bottoms
juice of 1/2 lemon
10 g tarragon and parsley
250 ml water
salt, pepper

Boil lobster in salted water for about ten minutes, let cool, and divide into two parts. Collect the fluid and creamy substance from the lobster's head. Melt 50 g of butter in a pan and add bacon. After the bacon has melted, remove it and put carrots, onions, artichoke bottoms, and lemon juice in the pan. Allow to cook for ten minutes over a low flame. Add 250 ml of water and allow to cook for another ten minutes. Remove the vegetables and allow the fluid to rest for a few minutes so that the fat on top can settle. Skim off the fat. Put the juices in a pan and reduce by half. In the meantime divide the lobster along its length, take out the meat, and cut it into pieces. Then cut up the artichoke bottoms into cubes. Add the rest of the butter (250 g) to the fluid and, on a low flame, beat with a whisk until it forms a creamy sauce. Add the lobster meat, the artichoke bottoms, and the vegetables, season with parsley and tarragon, add salt and pepper, and allow to cook for four minutes. Then put the lobster shell halves on a plate and fill them with the mixture. Garnish with parsley.

Vox

*Grand Hyatt Berlin
Marlene-Dietrich-Platz 2
(Tiergarten);
Potsdamer Platz subway
and S-Bahn station;
Tel. 25 53 17 32;
daily 12 noon to 2:30 p.m. and 6:30
p.m. to 10 p.m.;
Amex, Visa, Euro, Diners.*

Roasted Lamb Fillets on Mediterranean Vegetables

400 g lamb fillets	4 thin bread rolls
1 eggplant	100 g pesto
1 zucchini	100 ml balsamic
1 red and 1	vinegar
yellow pepper	200 ml olive oil
2 red onions	100 ml mutton
1 bunch of basil	juices
1 bunch of thyme	garlic

Bake eggplant, peppers and onions in the oven at 220° C. Season zucchini slices with salt and pepper and brown in olive oil. Remove peppers, eggplant, and zucchini from the oven, remove the skins and the seeds from the peppers. Cut vegetables into pieces 4 cm long and marinate with spices, fresh garlic and balsamic vinegar. Arrange marinated vegetables in the middle of the plate and place the bread rolls on top. When the lamb fillets have cooked until they are pink, place them on top of the vegetables and sprinkle with pesto and mutton juices.

Classic

Altes Zollhaus
*J 8 Carl-Hertz-Ufer 30
(Kreuzberg);
Prinzenstraße subway
station;
Tel. 692 33 00; Tuesday
through Saturday 6 p.m.
to 1 p.m.; all credit cards.*
An old customs house right next to the Landwehrkanal, with a landing for steamboats. Excellent German food in a rustic atmosphere.

Paris Bar
*E 7 Kantstrasse 152
(Charlottenburg);
Savignyplatz S-Bahn
station; Tel. 313 80 52;
daily 12 noon to 2 a.m.;
Amex.*
For 20 years this has been one of the nicest, most popular places among people who work in the areas of art, film or business. The

French food and the contemporary art on the walls are both of the highest quality.

Austrian-style café: Einstein

Einstein

G 7 *Kurfürstenstrasse 58 (Tiergarten); Nollendorfplatz subway station Tel. 261 50 96; daily 10 a.m. to 2 a.m.; Amex, Visa, Diners, Euro.*

Legendary café and restaurant in an old villa. Classic Austrian cuisine and freshly roasted coffee. When the weather is nice, you can sit outside under the fruit trees and enjoy the summer in the city.

Storch

F 9 *Wartburgstrasse 54 (Schöneberg); Eisenacher Strasse subway station; Tel. 784 20 59; Daily 6 p.m. to 1 a.m.; Master, Euro.*

Delicious Alsatian cuisine with crème caramel and choucroute (sauerkraut), served with appropriate wines at long wooden tables. You can't choose whom you sit with, but sometimes this can be entertaining.

Gourmet

Grand Slam

A 9 *Gottfried-von-Cramm-Weg 47-55 (Wilmersdorf); Grunewald S-Bahn station; Tel. 825 38 10; Tuesday through Saturday 6:30 p.m. to 12 p.m.; Amex, Visa, Euro, Diners.*

Located near the famous tennis club Rot-Weiss, Grand Slam is the domain of head cook Jürgen Fehrenbach, who always seems to serve up a winner, with an outstanding selection of wines and a Michelin star.

Vau

I 6 *Jägerstrasse 54-55 (Mitte); Hausvogteiplatz subway station; Tel. 202 97 30; Monday through Saturday from 12 noon; kitchen from 12 noon to 2:30 p.m. and 7 p.m. to 10:30 p.m.; Amex, Visa, Euro, Diners.*

Prominent people from the media scene meet here during the afternoon. The valuable

Calm before the storm: Vau

paintings exhibited on the walls change. The wine list is enormous, with 440 different offerings.

Bamberger Reiter

F 8 *Regensburger Strasse 7 (Schöneberg); Viktoria-Luise-Platz subway station; Tel. 218 42 82; Tuesday through Saturday 6 p.m. to 1 a.m.; Amex, Visa, Euro, Diners.*

Berlin's oldest gourmet restaurant also has a section for people with normal incomes; the food in the bistro is outstanding, but reasonably priced. Beautiful terrace.

Kaiserstuben

I 5 *In Kupfergraben 6a (Mitte); Friedrichstrasse subway and S-Bahn station; Tel. 20 45 29 80; Tuesday through Saturday 6 p.m. to 1 a.m.; Amex, Visa, Diners, Euro.*

Head cook Tim Raue is the star among Berlin's young chefs—partly because of his crazy ideas: one of his specialties is currywurst with french fries. The place only has seating for forty people, so make a reservation.

Hip

Cibo Matto

J 5 *Rosenthaler Strasse 44 (Mitte); Hackescher Markt subway station; Tel. 28 38 51 70; Sunday through Thursday 9 a.m. to 2 a.m., Friday, Saturday 9 a.m. to 4 a.m.; all credit cards.*

A favorite of young creative types in Mitte. Beautiful terrace in the courtyard. Italian food, with superb cocktails in the lounge.

Lubitsch

D 7 *Bleibtreustrasse 47 (Charlottenburg); Savignyplatz S-Bahn station; Tel. 885 12 94; Monday through Saturday 9:30 a.m. to 12 p.m.; Sunday from 5 p.m.; all credit cards.*

A pleasant restaurant with stucco, wood, and turquoise walls. Delicious, affordable food. All the meat is from an organic livestock dealer.

Joe Peña´s Casa Tres Kilos

I 9 *Marheinekeplatz 3 (Kreuzberg); Gneisenaustrasse subway station; Tel. 693 60 44; Sunday through Thursday 5 p.m. to 1 a.m., Friday, Saturday 5 p.m. to 2 a.m.; Amex, Visa, Master, Euro.*

Loud music, spicy food and superb margaritas. The terrace has a nice view of Kreuzberg.

Nola

F 5 *Dortmunder Strasse 9 (Moabit); Hansaplatz subway station; Tel. 399 69 69; Monday through Saturday 11 a.m. to 2 p.m., Sunday 10 a.m. to 2 a.m.; Amex, Visa, Euro.*

The fajitas are pure poetry. Chicken or scampi served hot and rolled in corn tortillas.

Kashmer Palace

F 8 *Marburger Strasse 14 (Charlottenburg); Augsburger Strasse subway station; Tel. 214 28 40; Tuesday through Friday 12 noon to 3 p.m. and 6 p.m. to 12 p.m., Saturday 12 noon to 12 p.m., Sunday 5 p.m. to 12 p.m.; Amex, Visa, Euro, Master, Diners.*

You'd have to go to London or Bombay to find better Indian cuisine. Tip: six types of bread (freshly baked), tandoori and mughlai.

Eating and Drinking outside

Summer in the city. What could be nicer than a cool Weizenbier in a pleasant beer garden?

Café am Neuen See

F 7 *Lichtensteinallee 1 (Tiergarten); Tiergarten or Zoo S-Bahn station, then ten minutes through Tiergarten; Tel. 254 49 30; winter 10 a.m. to 8 p.m., summer 10 a.m. to 11 p.m.; Amex, Euro, Visa.*

A taste of Munich right in the middle of Berlin. The city's best-loved beer garden is hidden amid the dense green foliage of Tiergarten.

Prater Garten

J 4 *Kastanienallee 7-9 (Prenzlauer Berg); Eberswalder Strasse subway station; Tel. 448 56 88; Monday through Friday from 2 PM, Saturday, Sunday from 12 noon, opens two hours later in the winter; no credit cards.*

An oasis of green in the middle of Prenzlauer Berg, this is the oldest beer garden in Berlin. The first beer was tapped 160 years ago.

Wirtshaus Moorlake

Wannsee *Moorlakeweg 1; Wannsee S-Bahn station + Bus 216; Tel. 805 58 09; Daily 10 a.m. to 6 p.m., open until 10 p.m. in the summer; all credit cards.*

This beer garden is 150 years old and is located by the park of the Klein-Glienicke castle. It has its own landing for boats and an excellent cultural program.

Blockhaus Nikolskoe

Wannsee *Nikolskoer Weg; S-Bahn station Wannsee + Bus 216; Tel. 805 29 14; Daily 10 a.m. to 6 p.m., (hot food served from 12 noon); summer 12 noon to 9 p.m.; no credit cards.*

The ideal place to stop during a weekend trip to the outskirts of town. Visitors can enjoy a good view over the Havel and Grunewald.

Good Friend

E 7 *Kantstrasse 30 (Charlottenburg); Savignyplatz S-Bahn station; Tel. 313 26 59; Monday through Sunday 12 noon to 2 a.m.; Amex, Euro, Visa, Master.*

The best Chinese food in Berlin. The proof: many Chinese families seen eating the excellent Cantonese cuisine here. The lobster dishes are yummy. Reservations are a good idea.

Fukagawa

E 8 *Pfalzburger Strasse 20 (Wilmersdorf); Hohenzollernplatz subway station; Tel. 873 72 95; Monday through Friday 12 noon to 3 a.m., daily 6 p.m. to 11 p.m.; Amex, Euro.*

A fine teppanyaki and sushi restaurant. A favorite among fashionable Russians, who like the atmosphere and the sake selection.

Sala Thai

C 6/7 *Kaiserdamm 112 (Charlottenburg); Sophie-Charlotte-Platz subway station; Tel. 322 48 80; Monday through Friday 6 p.m. to 12 p.m., Saturday, Sunday 12 noon to 12 p.m.; Amex, Visa, Diners, Euro.*

The biggest Thai restaurant in Berlin (180 seats). Traditional Thai dance on Wednesdays from 8 p.m. to 10 p.m.

Italian

XII Apostel

E 7 *Bleibtreustrasse 49 (Charlottenburg);*

Pizza and Pasta for popes: XII Apostel

Savignyplatz S-Bahn station; Tel. 312 14 33; daily 24 hours; no credit cards.

If the pope liked pizza, this would be his favorite restaurant in Berlin. Every pizza is named for an apostle. Big advantage: open 24 hours.

Trattoria Lappeggi

K 4 *Kollwitzstrasse 56 (Prenzlauer Berg), Senefelderplatz subway station; Tel. 442 63 47; daily from 12 noon, kitchen open until 12 p.m., Saturday and Sunday until 1 a.m.; Amex, Euro, Visa*

Hip meeting place in Prenzlauer Berg. Nice terrace with a view of Kollwitzplatz.

La Cascina

B 9 *Delbrückstrasse 17 (Wilmersdorf); Grunewald S-Bahn station; Tel. 826 17 9; Thursday through Tuesday 12 noon to 12 p.m.; Amex, Euro, Visa, Diners, Master.*

Rossini in Grunewald. A meeting place for the rich, famous and beautiful of West Berlin. Spoils you with everything that is good and expensive in Italy.

The large garden terrace is open in the summer.

Greek

Fou Fou

L 8 *Görlitzer Strasse 63 (Kreuzberg) Görlitzer Bahnhof subway station; Tel. 617 59 71; daily 4 p.m. to 2 a.m.; no credit cards.*

Fou Fou means "open fire." Many Kreuzbergers with a taste for Greek food come to warm themselves here.

Ypsilon

G 9 *Hauptstrasse 163 (Schöneberg); Kleistpark subway station; Tel. 782 45 39; daily from 5 p.m.; no credit cards.*

Popular Greek cuisine. Greeks of all ages meet here and mix with people from the neighborhood.

Vegetarian

Natural'Mente

C 6 *(In the Makro-Zentrum, Schusterrusstrasse 26; (Charlottenburg); Richard-Wagner-Platz subway station; Tel. 341 41 66; Monday 12 noon to 3 p.m., Tuesday through Friday 12 noon to 10 p.m., Saturday 6 p.m. to 10 p.m., Sunday 11 a.m. to 3 p.m.; no credit cards.*

Hakuin: Buddhist style

Macrobiotic food, but not for hardliners. Fresh fish. Excellent cake.

Hakuin
F 8 *Martin-Luther-Strasse 1a (Schöneberg); Wittenbergplatz subway station; Tel. 218 20 27; Tuesday through Friday 4 p.m. to 11:30 p.m., Saturday, Sunday 12 noon to 11:30 p.m.; closed Mondays; no credit cards.*

Even Buddhism has a price. The ambience and the food are of the highest quality, but this doesn't come cheap. Reservations required.

Abendmahl
L 8 *Muskauer Strasse 9 (Kreuzberg) Görlitzer Bahnhof subway station; Tel. 612 51 70 ; daily 6 p.m. to 1 a.m. (kitchen open until 11:30 p.m.); no credit cards.*

Vegetarian nouvelle cuisine: elegant dishes with ingredients from an organic farm. Also offers fish and a good selection of organic wines.

Fast food

Vietnam Bistro
J 4 *Weinbergweg 25 (Mitte); Rosenthaler Platz subway station; Tel. 449 58 96; Monday through Friday 11 a.m. to 12 p.m., Saturday, Sunday 12 noon to 1 a.m.*

An inexpensive neighborhood fast-food place with minimal furnishings. Simple Vietnamese dishes freshly prepared.

Salam Falafel
E 7/8 *Rankestrasse 3 (Charlottenburg); Kufürstendamm subway station; Tel. 881 34 61; Sunday through Thursday 11 a.m. to 2 a.m., Friday, Saturday 11 a.m. to 3 a.m.*

Mideastern specialties. Especially good: Arabic sweets like date cakes and cinnamon tea.

Piccola Romantica
K 8 *Oranienstrasse 33 (Kreuzberg); Kottbusser Tor subway station; Tel. 61 40 30 11; Sunday through Thursday 11 a.m. to 2 a.m., Friday, Saturday 11 a.m. to 3 a.m.*

More than a few people say that this is the best Italian fast food in Berlin. Excellent pasta and pizza. No seating.

Cheap

Shayan
G 8 *Goltzstrasse 23 (Schöneberg); Nollendorfplatz subway station; Tel. 215 15 47; Daily 12 noon to 12 p.m.; no credit cards.*

Persian specialties, all homemade. No seating. Especially good: "Bereschk Polo" and the vegetable cake.

La Musica
L 9 *Pannierstrasse 24 (Neukölln); Hermannplatz subway station; Tel. 623 60 73;*

daily 11 a.m. to 12 p.m.; no credit cards.

Cheap and delicious. Pizza and pasta for just DM 5.99 in pleasant Neukölln neighborhood atmosphere.

Sushi
D 8 *Pariser Strasse 44 (Wilmersdorf); Spichernstrasse subway station; Tel. 881 27 90 ; daily 12 noon to 12 p.m., Sunday 4 p.m. to 12 p.m. no credit cards.*

A small, elegant sushi restaurant. Experts should try the Japanese beer.

Cafés

Café am Ufer
L 8 *Paul-Lincke-Ufer 42-43 (Kreuzberg); Schön-leinstrasse subway station; Tel. 612 28 27; Daily 10 a.m. to 2 a.m.; Visa.*

Located on a bank of the Landwehrkanal in Kreuzberg, supposedly one of Berlin's hippest neighborhoods, Café am Ufer is where architects and people from nearby ad agencies come to spend their lunch hour.

TTT
G 9 *Goltzstrasse 2 (Schöneberg); Eisenacher Strasse subway stations; Tel. 21 75 22 40; Monday through Saturday 8:30 a.m. to 12 p.m., Sunday*

TTT: tea, tea, tea – 140 different kinds

PHOTO: Jörn Lehmann

Just like home?

Forget haute cuisine, and, for that matter, forget health too. Snackfood or Imbiss food is still a hit. There are more than 1,300 places to find Döner(kebabs) or currywurst in Berlin. These are the best:

Döner

Piliç Döner

D 7 *Krumme Strasse/ Wilmersdorfer Strasse (Charlottenburg); Wilmersdorfer Strasse; station; daily 10 a.m. to 3 a.m.*

Inconspicuous stand with delicious chicken döner from DM 1.99. Also the cheapest freshly squeezed orange juice in Berlin: one third of a liter for DM 2.50.

Döner

J 4 *Rosenthaler Strasse/ Brunnenstrasse (Mitte); Rosenthaler Platz subway station; daily 9 a.m. to 5 a.m.*

Döner culture has taken hold quickly in the eastern part of the city. This snack bar was one of the pioneers. Our recommendation: the veal döner.

Yeni Misir Capasi / Dürum Döner

K 8 *Adalbertstrasse 96 (Kreuzberg); Kottbusser Damm subway station; daily 9 a.m. to 5 a.m.*

Nights in Kreuzberg are long, and the neighborhood has standout döners. The best bet here is the chicken döner for DM 2.99.

Akarsu Imbiss

L 8 *Wiener Strasse 62 (Kreuzberg); Görlitzer Bahnhof subway station; Daily 9 a.m. to 5 a.m.*

A small snack stand right next to the Morena Bar, which is why the dawn closing is particularly important. Döners from DM 2.50, served in freshly baked bread.

Currywurst

Schnellimbiss

E 7 *Savignyplatz/Carmerstrasse (Charlottenburg); Savignyplatz S-Bahn station; Monday through Friday 9 a.m. to 6 p.m.*

Full to bursting in the afternoon, when media and management types come for the curry-wurst and hamburgers. The chef makes the ketchup from a secret recipe.

Curry 36

I 8 *Mehringdamm 36 (Kreuzberg); Mehringdamm subway station; daily from 10 a.m. until the early hours of the morning.*

Order the delicious currywurst "with" or "without" skin: you still get the best tomato ketchup in the city.

Bachhuber's bei Wittys

F 7 *Wittenbergplatz (Schöneberg); Wittenbergplatz subway station; Monday through Saturday 11 a.m. to 12:30 p.m., Sunday 11 a.m. to 11:30 p.m.*

The meat for the sausages comes from the famous Bachhuber butcher's shop, ensuring high quality. And the oil for the french fries is changed every day, which makes a big difference in the taste.

Biers Kudamm 195

E 7 *Kurfürstendamm 195 (Charlottenburg); Savignyplatz S-Bahn station; Daily 11 a.m. to 5 a.m., Sunday from 12 a.m.*

To the employees of Berlin's best-known currywurst stand, everyone is equal: taxi drivers, sleepless techno fans and yuppies. People with more elegant tastes are also catered to: they can eat their curry with champagne (Moet & Chandon) served in a proper glass.

10 a.m. to 12 p.m.; Visa. Berlin's first tea salon offers 140 different types of tea served in a pleasant atmosphere. The specialty is green tea.

Strandbad Mitte
I 5 *Kleine Hamburger Strasse 16 (Mitte); Weinmeisterstrasse subway station; Tel. 280 84 03; daily 9 a.m. to 2 a.m.; no credit cards.*
The name, which means "Beach Mitte" is deceptive; no one starts swimming here until the fourth vodka-lemon. Scene café in Mitte.

Morena Bar
L 8 *Wiener Strasse 60 (Kreuzberg); Görlitzer Bahnhof subway station; Tel. 618 80 13; Daily 9 a.m. to 4 p.m.; no credit cards.*
A classic, but unfortunately it's always full. Specials: Spanish breakfast (pancakes with maple syrup and fresh fruit), or Dutch breakfast (peanut butter, apricot marmalade, and chocolate streusel).

Barcomi's Deli
J 5 *Sophienstrasse 21 (Mitte); Weinmeisterstrasse subway station; Tel. 28 59 83 63; Monday through Saturday 9 a.m.*

Monster bagles at Barcomi's Deli

to 10 p.m., Sunday from 10 a.m.; no credit cards.
Excellent café with American character. Attracts a hip young crowd. The coffees are gigantic, and so are the monster bagels.

Anita Wronski
K 4 *Knaackstrasse 26-28 (Prenzlauer Berg); Eberswalder Strasse subway station; Tel. 442 84 83; Monday through Friday 9 a.m. to 2 a.m., Saturday, Sunday 10 a.m. to 3 a.m.; no credit cards.*
Yet another scene bar, with student prices. Serves breakfast until 3.

Look at this city!
It must be the height: if you like a nice view when you're eating, you should try one of these restaurants:

Grunewaldturm
Grunewald *Havelchaussee 61; Theodor-Heuss-Platz subway station; Tel. 304 12 03; Daily 10 a.m. to 12 p.m.; Visa, Amex, Euro.*
The tower, which is fifty-six meters tall, was built over one hundred years ago on top of the Karlsberg hill, which is seventy-seven meters tall. From here you have a fantastic view of the Havel. The food is good too.

Tabuna
F 5 *Alt-Moabit 59; Turmstrasse subway station; Tel. 390 70 40; Daily 12 noon to 12 p.m.; no credit cards.*
The terrace has a nice view of the Spree and the surrounding buildings. Middle Eastern-Mediterranean cuisine.

Restaurant in the Radio Tower
A 7 *Hammarskjöldplatz; Theodor-Heuss-Platz subway station; Tel. 30 38 29 96; Tuesday through Sunday 10 a.m. to 11 p.m.; Amex, Euro, Visa.*
Panoramic view 55 meters above the ground. The radio tower is 138 meters high, and the elevator to the observation deck runs from 10 a.m. to 9 p.m.

Restaurant in the TV Tower
J 5 *Am Alexanderplatz; Alexanderplatz subway and S-Bahn station; Tel. 242 33 33 ; Daily 10 a.m. to 12 p.m.; all credit cards.*
A high point among Berlin restaurants, both literally and figuratively. The rotating restaurant is 207 meters above the ground, and the TV tower is 365 meters high. German cuisine.

In the summer you can bask in the sun by the water tower.

Lunch

Bovril
D 8 *Kurfürstendamm 184 (Charlottenburg); Adenauer Platz subway station; Tel. 881 84 61; daily 10 a.m. to 2 a.m.; Amex, Visa, Diners, Euro.*

In the summer you can dawdle on the beautiful terrace, relax after a walk along Kurfürstendamm. Prices for the lunch menu start at DM 23.

Galeries Lafayette
I 6 *Französische Strasse 23 (Mitte); Französische Strasse subway station; Tel. 20 94 80; Monday through Friday 9:30 a.m. to 8 p.m., Saturday 9:30 a.m. to 4 p.m.; Amex, Visa, Diners, Euro.*

In the basement you can dine just like in Paris. (Even the prices have a French flavor.) Still, the food is delicious.

Late night food

Bagels + Bialys
J 5 *Rosenthaler Strasse 46-48 (Mitte); Hackescher Markt S-Bahn station; Tel. 283 65 46; daily 9 a.m. to 4 a.m.; no credit cards.*

Real bagels from New York and homemade schawarmas until the early hours of the morning.

Ali Baba
D 7 *Bleibtreustrasse 45 (Charlottenburg); Savignyplatz S-Bahn*

station; Tel. 881 13 50; Daily 11:30a.m. to 3 a.m.; Visa.

The best minipizza in Berlin, for DM 2. Attracts mostly a young crowd, but in the afternoon business people come to eat pizza and pasta. Rustic atmosphere.

Habibi: Chick-peas and fresh juice

Habibi
G 8 *Goltzstrasse 24 (Schöneberg); Nollendorfplatz subway station; Tel. 215 33 22; Daily 11 a.m. to 3 a.m., Friday, Saturday until 5 a.m.; no credit cards.*

Serves some of the tastiest falafels in Berlin. The freshly squeezed juices are another highlight.

Schwarzes Café
E 7 *Kantstrasse 148 (Charlottenburg); Savignyplatz S-Bahn station; Tel. 313 80 38; daily 24 hours; no credit cards.*

Breakfast whenever you want or a late-night dinner at four in the morning—no problem, anything is possible here. The beautiful garden is open in the summer. The toilets are also interesting enough to deserve a look.

Ice cream

Florida
Spandau Klosterstrasse 15; Rathaus Spandau subway station; Tel. 331 56 66; daily 12 noon to 11 p.m.; no credit cards.

It might be a long way to Spandau, but in this case it's worth the trip. Our favorite: chocolate.

Eiscafé Mohnheim
D 9 *Blissestrasse 12 (Wilmersdorf); Blissestrasse subway station; Tel. 822 86 32; daily 10 a.m. to 6 p.m. (closed in the winter).*

Homemade ice cream. A family business, with the best ice cream in Berlin. Our favorite: rhubarb and cinnamon.

Häagen-Dazs
E 7 *Kurfürstendamm 224 (Charlottenburg); Kurfürstendamm subway station; Tel. 882 12 07; Sunday through Thursday 12 noon to 11 p.m., Friday, Saturday 11 a.m. to 11 p.m.*

Everyone's favorite ice cream has its own shop, with very pleasant service and a clean, bright atmosphere.

Häagen Dazs: Ice cream on Ku'damm

A room with

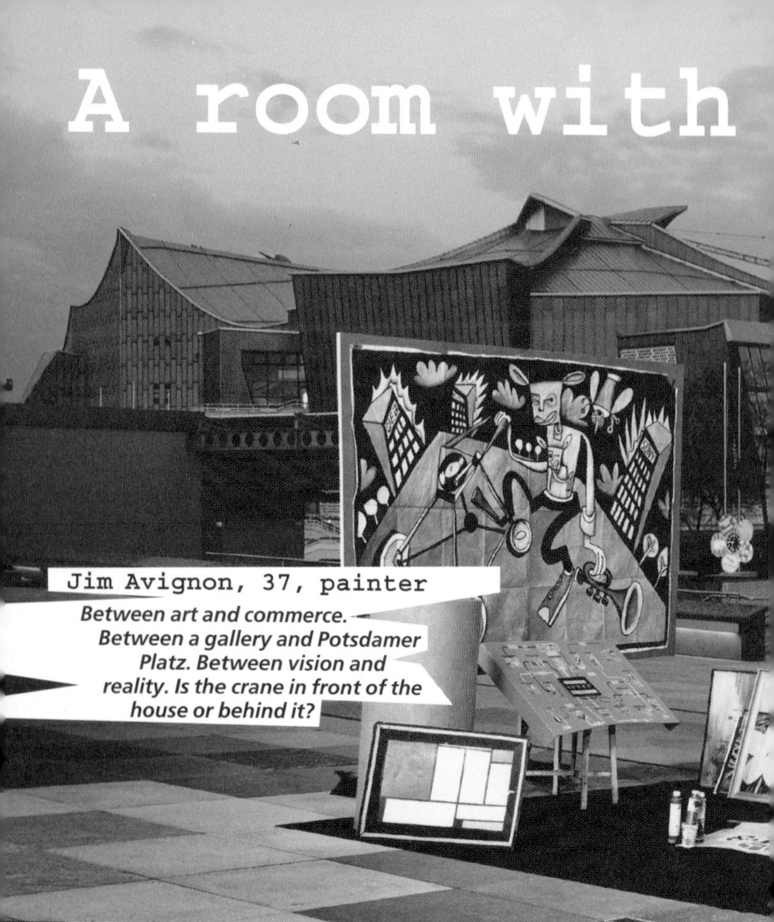

Jim Avignon, 37, painter

*Between art and commerce.
Between a gallery and Potsdamer
Platz. Between vision and
reality. Is the crane in front of the
house or behind it?*

**Mitja Prinz, 26,
disc jockey**

*Tower blocks and house music,
too cold on Alexanderplatz*

**Töchter + Söhne, 13 months,
PR agency**

*Pack up your bathing suit,
take your young daughter, and
come with us to Wannsee…*

a View

Someone pulls the rug out from under your feet and throws you out in the cold. Töchter + Söhne, a student PR agency from HdK Berlin (Berlin's Fine Arts College), puts young people and their living rooms out on the street.
Photos: Nico Hesselmann/Z 21

I n the spring of 1998 some people studying at the Berliner Hochschule der Künste (Berlin's Fine Arts College) started the first student PR agency in Germany, which is called Töchter und Söhne (Daughters and Sons). Since then, more than one hundred new recruits have worked together on the development of ad campaigns, web sites, PR strategies, film productions, cartoon series, and new formats for TV broadcasting. The control center is a former atelier in the school's main building. The space serves as a combined reception area, conference room, graphics department, management floor, coffee room, bookkeeping department, and production area. The students improvise on how a PR agency should be run, with clients like Otto-Versand, ProSieben, Hertha BSC, and Berlin's AIDS awareness program.

The unconventional has been elevated to a guiding principle: a meeting with a client is scheduled between two lectures, agency representatives ride to presentations on bikes, and business lunches are held in the student dining hall. This way the students are able to gain practical experience while still in school.

Töchter + Söhne works like an outside partner providing fresh insight and new ways of seeing. The students provide ideas and creativity, and established agencies follow through with production and realization.

The students are supported by businesses from many areas in the communications field. They are honorary members of Töchter + Söhne's board of trustees, ready either to help the agency directly or to provide good advice. The list of partners has grown to more than twenty, including Springer & Jacoby, Scholz & Friends, Pixelpark and the Babelsberg film studio. For more information: HYPERLINK mailto:ts@hdk-berlin.de

Budget

Die Fabrik
M 8 *Schlesische Strasse 18, 10997 Berlin (Kreuzberg); Schlesisches Tor subway station; Tel. 611 71 16; Fax 618 29 74; www.diefabrik.com; single rooms from DM 66, doubles DM 94, 3 beds DM 120, 4 beds DM 144; no credit cards.*
This building was a factory at the turn of the last century, but it has been renovated. Furnishings are simple, with communal showers and toilets.

Studentenhotel
F 9 *Meininger Strasse 10, 10823 Berlin (Schöneberg); Rathaus Schöneberg subway station; Tel. 784 67 20; Fax 788 15 23; single rooms DM 60, doubles DM 44, 4 beds DM 40 (per person, including breakfast); no credit cards.*
Centrally located in Schöneberg. Simple furnishings, with bathrooms and showers in the hall.

Nina, Cedric and Sascha, 74, roommates
Egg chairs found on the street and spaghetti Bolognese

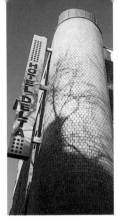

**Hotel Delta:
sun and comfort**

Hotel am Anhalter Bahnhof
I 7 *Stresemannstrasse 36, 10963 Berlin (Kreuzberg); Hallesches Tor subway station; Tel. 251 03 42; Fax 251 48 97; single rooms from DM 80, doubles from DM 110 (including breakfast); Visa, Euro.*

Not far from Potsdamer Platz. The amenities vary from room to room; some have their own toilets and showers, others share facilities down the hall. Radio, television, and telephone in some rooms.

Juncker's Hotel Garni
M 6 *Grünberger Strasse 21, 10243 Berlin (Friedrichshain); Frankfurter Tor subway station Tel. 293 35 50; Fax 29 33 55 55; single rooms from DM 115, doubles from DM 130 (breakfast for an additional DM 10); Euro, Visa.*

Good value for the money. All rooms have shower and toilet, telephone, and TV. Excellent location right in the middle of Friedrichshain.

Delta Hotel Berlin
G 8 *Pohlstrasse 58, 10785 Berlin (Tiergarten); Kurfürstenstrasse or Nollendorfplatz subway station; Tel. 26 00 20; Fax 26 00 21 11; E-mail: Delta.Hotel.Berlin@t-online.de; single rooms from DM 150, doubles from DM 204; Visa, Amex, Diners, Euro.*

A charming hotel in a quiet location between Kurfürstenstrasse and Potsdamer Platz. Well-furnished rooms and a pleasant sun terrace.

Hotel Albatros: art, TV, and telephones for everyone

Albatros Hotel
D 9 *Rudolstädter Strasse 42, 10713 Berlin (Wilmersdorf); Heidelberger Platz subway and S-Bahn station; Tel. 89 78 30; Fax 89 78 31 00; single rooms from DM 120, doubles from DM 195 (including breakfast); Amex, Diners, Euro, Visa.*

Good value for the money. All rooms have televisions and telephones, but some have showers and toilets in the hall.

Hotel Carmer 16
E 7 *Carmerstrasse 16 , 10623 Berlin (Charlottenburg); Savignyplatz S-Bahn station; Tel. 31 10 05 00; Fax 31 10 05 10; Single rooms from DM 130 (DM 80 without shower), doubles from DM 160 (DM 120 without shower); Diners, Visa, Euro, Amex.*

Only five minutes from Kurfürstendamm, this is a good place to stay if you're planning on some late nights in West Berlin. The low-budget rooms are fine, too.

Frauenhotel Artemisia
D 8 *Brandenburgische Strasse 18, 10707 Berlin (Wilmersdorf) Konstanzer Strasse subway station; Tel. 873 89 05 ; Fax 861 86 53; E-mail: frauenhotel-berlin@t-online.de; double rooms from DM 170; Visa, Euro, Amex.*

The name should be an indication: no men allowed. In the summer women have the roof terrace all to themselves.

ibis
K 5 *Prenzlauer Allee 4, 10405 Berlin (Prenzlauer Berg); Alexanderplatz subway and S-Bahn station; Tel. 44 33 30; Fax 44 33 31 11; single/double room DM 133 (breakfast for an additional DM 15); Amex, Visa, Euro, Diners.*

Simple and engaging. Great weekend prices, beginning at DM 99.

Adlon oblige

The building is shrouded in legends. Now the Adlon is back—on the way to becoming one of Berlin's most prestigious addresses.

Albert Einstein, Charie Chaplin, Thomas Mann, and Greta Garbo were among the guests. Marlene Dietrich was discovered here. The hotel, opened by Lorenz Adlon in 1907 on Pariser Platz, was one of the most beautiful in the world. At the end of World War II the Red Army plundered the wine cellar and set the building on fire. After years of arguments, the name Adlon was finally revived in 1997. But critics say that all the new hotel has in common with the old Adlon is its location and its name. The only thing that remains from the original hotel is the fountain in the entry hall, which an excavator dug up somewhere. Still, the old motto, *Adlon oblige* ("Adlon at your service"), remains as true as ever. A foyer with a brilliant glass dome, spacious rooms with subdued art deco furnishings, and—not to be scoffed at—heated towel racks in every bathroom.

Hotel Adlon

I 6 *Unter den Linden 77, 10117 Berlin; Tel. 22 61-0; Reservations Tel. 22 61 11 11; Fax 22 61 22 22; www.hotel-adlon.de.* The most affordable accommodation here for one person in the "executive" category would be a room on the second or third floor for DM 440. The Presidential Suite for heads of state and other people "requiring protection" (an official classification) costs DM 5,300 a night. (The windows are bulletproof.) The Adlon has 337 rooms, including 51 suites.

Seehof am Lietzensee

C 7 *Lietzenseeufer 11 14057 Berlin (Charlottenburg); Sophie-Charlotte-Platz subway station; Tel. 32 00 20; Fax 32 00 22 51; single room DM 238, double DM 298 (including breakfast); Amex, Visa, Euro, Diners.* A comfortable, smaller hotel near the Exhibition Center. Most

rooms have a view of the Lietzensee.

Berlin Hilton

I 6 *Mohrenstrasse 30, 10117 Berlin (Mitte); Hausvogteiplatz subway station; Tel. 202 30; Fax 20 23 42 69; www.hilton.com; single rooms from DM 245; Amex, Visa, Euro, Diners.* A modern glass building located right in

the middle of Berlin's new center. Galeries Lafayette, Planet Hollywood, and Quartier 206 are all within walking distance.

Alexander Plaza Berlin

J 5 *Rosenstrasse 1, 10178 Berlin (Mitte); Hachescher Markt S-Bahn* station; Tel. 24 00 10; Fax 24 00 17 77; www.alexander-plaza.com; single rooms from DM 255, doubles from DM 285; Amex, Visa, Euro, Diners.

Now under new management, which has brought some refreshing changes. The hotel is right across from the RTL TV station's main studio on Alexanderplatz, which could be an advantage for people interested in the German media scene.

Hecker's Hotel

E 7 Grolmanstrasse 35, 10625 Berlin (Charlottenburg); Uhlandstrasse subway station Tel. 889 00; Fax 889 02 60; www.heckers-hotel.com; single rooms from DM 230, doubles from DM 280 (not including breakfast); Amex, Visa, Euro, Diners.

Regular customers love the familiar atmosphere. The average size of the rooms is thirty-five square meters, and the furniture is all Italian design. A good restaurant, Cassambalis, lies adjacent to the hotel.

The Westin Grand

I 6 Friedrichstrasse 158-164, 10117 Berlin (Mitte); Französische Strasse subway station, Friedrichstrasse S-Bahn station; Tel. 202 70 ; Fax 20 27 33 62; www.westin-grand.com; single rooms from DM 265, doubles from DM 305 (not including breakfast); Amex, Visa, Euro, Diners.

New luxury in the east,

Within stumbling distance of The Paris Bar: the Savoy Hotel

located between Quartier 206 and Galeries Lafayette. Spacious rooms with interiors inspired by eighteenth-century décor. Extras: swimming pool, sauna, whirlpool, and massage.

Savoy Hotel

E 7 Fasanenstrasse 9-10, 10623 Berlin (Charlottenburg); Zoo subway and S-Bahn station; Tel. 31 10 30; Fax 31 10 33 33; www.savoy-hotels.com; single rooms from DM 249, doubles from DM 289; Amex, Visa, Euro, Diners.

A legend in the center of West Berlin, not far from the equally legendary Paris Bar. Kurfürstendamm and the Theater des Westens are within walking distance. Herbanos Bar, which is part of the hotel, is very good.

Hotel Hackescher Markt

J 5 Grosse Präsidentenstrasse 8,

10178 Berlin (Mitte); Hackescher Markt S-Bahn station; Tel. 28 00 30; Fax 28 00 31 11; single rooms from DM 180, doubles from DM 220; Amex, Visa, Euro, Diners.

This small jewel on Hackescher Markt proves that new buildings can be charming, too. Serious, dignified atmosphere.

Alsterhof Ringhotel

F 8 Augsburger Strasse 5 10789 Berlin (Charlottenburg); Augsburger Strasse subway station; Tel. 21 24 20 ; Fax 21 83 94 59; www.top-hotel.de/alster-hof; single rooms from DM 185, doubles from DM 230 (including breakfast); Amex, Visa, Euro, Diners.

Ideal location in the west: KaDeWe and Kurfürstendamm are just a short walk away.

Estrel Residence & Congress Hotel

M 11 Sonnenallee 225; 12057 Berlin (Neukölln); Sonnenallee S-Bahn station; Tel. 683 10; Fax 68 31 23 45; www.estrel.com; singles and doubles from DM 165; Amex, Visa, Euro, Diners.

Old charm in a new setting: Hotel Hackescher Markt

The biggest hotel in Germany, with 1,125 rooms. The Estrel is like a self-contained world, with its own restaurants and shops.

Designer Hotels

Ritz Carlton Schlosshotel Vier Jahreszeiten (Four Seasons)

A 10 *Brahmsstrasse 10, 14193 Berlin (Grunewald); Halenseen S-Bahn station; Tel. 89 58 40; Fax 89 58 48 00; www.ritzcarlton.com; rooms from DM 555; Amex, Visa, Euro, Diners.*

Design by Karl Lagerfeld, who has been provided with a room here for the rest of his life. Romy Schneider celebrated her wedding here.

Sorat Art'Otel Berlin

E 7 *Joachimstaler Strasse 28/29 10719 Berlin (Charlottenburg); Kurfürstendamm subway station; Tel. 88 44 70; Fax 88 44 77 00; www.sorat-hotels.com; single rooms from DM 235, doubles from DM 275; Amex, Visa, Euro, Diners.*

A hotel that feels like a gallery, right on Kurfürstendamm.
Avant-garde design and art by Wolf Vostell.

Art'Otel Ermelerhaus

J 6 *Wallstrasse 70-73, 10179 Berlin (Mitte); Klosterstrasse subway station; Tel. 24 06 20; Fax 24 06 22 22; www.arto-tel.de; single rooms from 235 DM (including breakfast); Amex, Visa, Euro, Diners.*

An unusual marriage of the Ermelerhaus, a state monument, and the latest in modern architecture. The building is dedicated to the artist Georg Baselitz.

Luxury

Kempinski Bristol

E 7 *Kurfürstendamm 27, 10719 Berlin (Charlottenburg); Kurfürstendamm subway station; Tel. 88 43 40; Fax 883 60 75; www.kempinski.com;*

Art comes to life: Art'Otel Ermelerhaus

single rooms from DM 365, doubles from DM 425 (including breakfast); Amex, Visa, Euro, Diners.

Traditional luxury hotel on Kurfürstendamm.
The finest furnishings, in the English style.
Some former guests: Sir Peter Ustinov, Mikhail Gorbachev, Mick Jagger, Bruce Willis.

Grand Hyatt Berlin

H 7 *Marlene-Dietrich-Platz 2, 10785 Berlin (Mitte); Potsdamer Platz subway and S-Bahn station; Tel. 25 53 12 34; Fax 25 53 12 35; www.hyatt.com; single rooms from DM 420; Amex, Visa, Euro, Diners.*

The first Hyatt in Europe, with 325 luxurious rooms, five stars, two presidential suites, etc., etc. The building was designed by the Spanish architect José Rafael Moneo, while the Swiss architect Hannes Wettstein designed the interiors.

Bleibtreu Hotel

D 8 *Bleibtreustrasse 31, 10707 Berlin (Charlottenburg); Savignyplatz S-Bahn station; Tel. 88 47 40; Fax 88 47 44 44; www.bleib-treu.com; single rooms from DM 275, doubles from DM 345 (including breakfast); Amex, Visa, Euro, Diners.*

The nearby Bleibtreustrasse is home to a row of designer shops and other small, exclusive stores. The grandiose inner courtyard has an Italian feel.

Inter-Continental

F 7 *Budapester Strasse 2, 10787 Berlin (Charlottenburg); Zoo subway and S-Bahn station; Tel. 260 20; Fax 26 02 11 82; www.inter-conti.com single rooms from DM 365, doubles from DM 415; Amex, Visa, Euro, Diners.*

Where Bill Clinton and other official guests stay during visits to Berlin.
A luxurious building in the American style, right by Tiergarten.

Fancy a bath?
Bleibtreu Hotel

Four Seasons Hotel
I 6 *Charlottenstrasse 49, 10117 Berlin (Mitte); Französische Strasse subway station; Tel. 203 38; Fax 20 33 61 66; single rooms from DM 560, doubles from DM 645 (not including breakfast); Amex, Visa, Euro, Diners.*

What is luxury, anyway? Good question. The Four Seasons: deep marble baths on seven floors, open fireplaces, an outstanding restaurant, and a posh address on the Gendarmenmarkt.

Kurfürst Hotel Pension
D 8 *Bleibtreustrasse 34, 10707 Berlin (Charlottenburg); Savignyplatz S-Bahn station; Tel. 885 68 20; Fax 883 13 76; E-mail: info@kurfuerst.com; single rooms from DM 140, doubles from DM 170; Amex, Diners, Euro, Visa.*

23 rooms with showers and nice furnishings.

Hotel-Pension Imperator
E 7 *Meinekestrasse 5 10719 Berlin (Charlottenburg);*

Kurfürstendamm subway station; Tel. 881 41 81; Fax 885 19 19; single rooms from DM 100, doubles from DM 160; no credit cards.

A beautifully maintained old building. Five-minute walk from Kurfürstendamm.

Hotel-Pension Kastanienhof
J 4 *Kastanienallee 65, 10119 Berlin (Prenzlauer Berg); Eberswalder Strasse subway station; Tel. 44 30 50; Fax 44 30 51 11; single rooms from DM 130, doubles from DM 170; Euro, Visa.*

An old Berlin house with the comforts of a hotel, including a bar. Also rents bicycles.

Pension Kreuzberg
I 8 *Großbeerenstrasse 64, 10963 Berlin (Kreuzberg); Mehringdamm subway station; Tel. 251 13 62; Fax 251 06 38; single rooms from DM 70, doubles from DM 95; no credit cards*

Thirteen large, spacious rooms of simple comfort, right in the heart of Kreuzberg.

Hotel-Pension Merkur
J 5 *Torstrasse 156, 10117 Berlin (Mitte); Rosenthaler Platz subway station; Tel. 282 82 97; Fax 282 77 65; single rooms from DM 65, doubles from DM 90; Amex, Diners, Euro, Visa.*

Central location not far from the Scheunenviertel. Simple and informal, and therefore not so expensive.

Jugendherberge Ernst Reuter
Reinickendorf Hermsdorfer Damm 48-50, 13467 Berlin; Hermsdorf S-Bahn station; Tel. 40 41 610; Fax 404 59 72; E-mail: jh-ernst-reuter@jugendher-berge.de; DM 28 for anyone under twenty-seven years old, otherwise DM 35 (including breakfast); no credit cards.

Very beautiful location in the Tegeler Fliess nature preserve.

Genuine imperial style: Hotel-Pension Imperator

Jugendgästehaus Berlin
G 7 *Kluckstrasse 3, 10785 Berlin (Tiergarten), Kurfürstenstrasse subway station, Tel. 261 10 97/8, Fax 265 03 83, DM 35 for anyone under twenty-seven, otherwise DM 42 DM (including breakfast); no credit cards.*

Trendy '60s architecture, a bar on the premises, and a central location in Tiergarten.

Fabulous location:
Schlosshotel
Cecilienhof

Jugendgästehaus Nordufer

Wedding *Norddufer 28, 13351 Berlin; Westhafen subway station; Tel. 45 19 91 12; Fax 452 41 00; E-mail: Norddufer@t-online.de; bed DM 37.50 (including breakfast); no credit cards.*

Not far from the beach at Plötzensee. Nicely furnished rooms.

Jugendgästehaus Central

E 8 *Nikolsburger Strasse 2-4, 10717 Berlin (Wilmersdorf); Hohenzollerndamm subway station; Tel. 873 01 88; Fax 861 34 85; www.jugendgaeste-haus.central.com beds from DM 38 (including breakfast); no credit cards.*

Large, well-lit rooms, only ten minutes from Kurfürstendamm.

Jugendherberge am Wannsee

Zehlendorf *Badeweg 1, 14129 Berlin; Nikolassee S-Bahn station; Tel. 803 20 35; Fax 803 59 08; www.jugendherberge.de;*

DM 34 for anyone under twenty-seven years old, otherwise DM 42 (including breakfast); no credit cards.

Located right by Wannsee. All the rooms have four beds.

In the country

Jagdschloss Hubertusstock

Kreis Barnim
Seerandstrasse 1, 16247 Joachimsthal/Hubertus-stock; Tel. 033363/500; Fax 033363/502 55; Amex, Diners, Euro, Visa.

A tradional castle located in the Schorheide, forty kilometers from the center of Berlin. Frederick the Great loved the guest house, and Erich Honecker would receive official guests here back in the days of the GDR.

Schlosshotel Cecilienhof

Potsdam *Neuer Garten, 14469 Potsdam; Tel. 0331/370 50; Fax 0331/29 24 98; www. castle-cecilienhof.com; single rooms/doubles from DM 195; Amex, Diners, Euro, Visa.*

Fantastic country seat in the English half-timbered style. Surrounded by trees, with a uniquely beautiful atmosphere.

Seidler Art'Otel Potsdam

Potsdam *Zeppelinstrasse 136, 17471 Potsdam; Tel. 0331/981 50; Fax 0331/981 55 55; www.ar-totel.de/potsdam; single rooms from DM 195, doubles from DM 215 (including breakfast); Amex, Diners, Euro, Visa.*

A modern glass palace with 123 rooms and suites, located right in the center of Potsdam.

Campingplatz am Krossinsee
Köpenick *Wernsdorfer Strasse 38; 12527 Berlin; Tel. 675 86 87; Fax 675 91 50; no credit cards; open year round.*

Campingplatz Dreilinden
Zehlendorf Albrechts *Teerofen 44, 14109 Berlin; Tel. 805 12 01; no credit cards; open from March 1 to October 31.*

Campingplatz Kladow
Spandau *Krampnitzer Weg 111-117, 14089 Berlin; Tel. 365 27 97; Fax 365 12 45; no credit cards; open year round.*

Agentur Wohnwitz
E 9 *Holsteinische Strasse 55, 10717 Berlin (Wilmersdorf); Blissestrasse subway station; Tel. 861 82 22; Fax 861 82 72; Monday through Friday 10 a.m to 7 p.m., Saturday 11 a.m. to 2 p.m.; no credit cards.*

Mitwohnzentrale
G 8 *Yorckstrasse 52, 10965 Berlin (Kreuzberg); Mehringdamm subway station; Tel. 194 30; Fax 216 94 01; www.mit-wohnzentrale.de; Monday through Friday 10 a.m. to 7 p.m.; no credit cards.*

Casa Nostra
G 8 *Winterfeldtstrasse 46, 10781 Berlin (Schöneberg); Nollendorfplatz subway station; Tel. 235 51 20; Fax 23 55 12 12; Monday through Friday 10 a.m. to 8 p.m., Saturday 11 a.m. to 3 p.m.; Euro, Visa.*

How do countries live?

Embassies from other countries are moving to Berlin along with the German government

The Russians were lucky. They can use the old Soviet Embassy on Unter den Linden. The enormous building went up during the 1950s with typical Stalinist bombast. A baroque structure with a heavily decorated façade, columns, and sculptures that immitate feudal palaces. The United States, Great Britain, and France are returning to their former addresses, but the old buildings are no longer up to the task of accommodating them, since the embassies in Bonn were much bigger. For this reason, investors are being sought to build expensive new embassies near Brandenburger Tor or on Unter den Linden.

The embassies in Pankow seem less representative of their tenants. In the days of East Germany, most of the embassies of the "socialist brother countries" were located in the conservative neighborhood near Schloss Niederschönhausen. Identical three-story structures were used to ensure that everyone was treated equally. The only difference was the flag in the front garden. After the Wall came down many of the buildings changed owners, and embassy staffs were reduced. Some of the poorer countries now only occupy the basements.

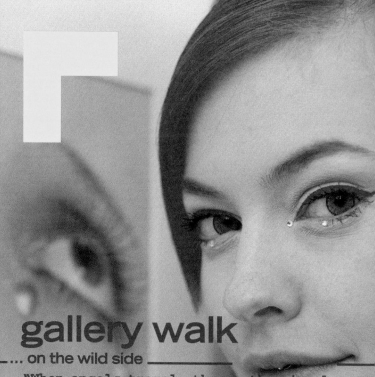

gallery walk
... on the wild side

"When angels travel, the weather is always nice," Enie van de Meiklokjes's grandmother used to say. Suddenly the sun is shining over Berlin. If angels have bright red hair, then Enie, a radio VJ at Viva, must be one. Volker Diehl, the founder of the prestigious "art forum" art fair, is convinced that she is. Enie is looking for a boyfriend, an intellectual, who has to have glasses. Unfortunately Volker doesn't wear any, so we will join Enie on her search. On the way we'll have a look at Berlin's art scene

Text by Caroline von der Tann, Photos by Quentin Ehmer

The sheer number of galleries in Berlin can lead to confusion. At last count there were about 300 of them. Of these, about 20 deserve to be taken seriously. The established dinosaurs are in Charlottenburg. Galleries in Mitte offer a better view of what's young and "in." The Berliner Kunstkalender (Berlin Art Calendar) contains listings of current shows.

02 The list of the artists represented at **Haas & Fuchs** reads like a Who's Who of modern art. Along with Grosz and Bacon there are also works by living legends like Hockney and Baselitz. Enie thinks the Baselitz paintings are dreadful: "When cats paint, they paint upside down." (She usually paints poodles. It only takes five minutes.)

01 The photo-gallery **Camera Work.** (Enie would like to live here and sell the pictures she takes with her Polaroid SX 70, which is covered with dark red leather. Of course she would sell them for $2, 500 each, like Helmut Newton.) There is no shortage of big names here: Helmut Newton, Sarah Moon, Irving Penn, Leni Riefenstahl. Gert Elfering's collection, which is worth millions, makes first-class exhibitions possible here.

02

EORG BASELITZ

03 In 1991, when most people at galleries were thinking more about survival than founding new ones, Thomas Schulte came from New York to Berlin and set up a gallery on Mommsenstrasse. With international artists like Richard Artschwager, Rebecca Horn, and Robert Mapplethorpe, **Franck + Schulte** managed to set new standards for the city, which before then had been rather provincial when it came to art dealing.

04 In 1997 Esther Schipper and Michael Krome moved from Cologne, bringing their **Galerie Schipper und Krome** along with them. The gallery is set up in a former liquor factory on Auguststrasse, and primarily features the works of artists who deal with contemporary communications technology and media, like Angela Bulloch, Philippe Parreno, and Matti Braun.

06 The one stumbling block at **Contemporary Fine Arts**: the small stairway that leads up into art heaven. In 1996 the gallery moved from Charlottenburg to Mitte. Here the trails are still fresh, and there is little need to worry about previous generations, according to Nicole Hackert, who runs the gallery. The first exhibition here in 1996, by the artist Sarah Lucas, bore the optimistic title: "Is suicide genetic?"

05 A dark industrial courtyard in Sophiestrasse: **Magnus von Plessen's Atelier.** The thirty-one-year-old autodidact used to work for the film producer Regina Ziegler. Three years ago he had his breakthrough with an exhibition at Hackesche Höfe. In the meantime he has also made an appearance at "art forum," but what he likes more than anything is showing up in his grandfather's old pinstripe suit. His main theme is the isolation of the individual in late capitalism. He likes lollipops. (But unfortunately doesn't wear glasses.)

08 In September 1998 **Galerie Neugeriemschneider** moved from Charlottenburg with its brand new iMacs, settling in at Linienstrasse 155. Although they were outsiders when they started, Burkhard Riemschneider (a former editor at Taschen Verlag Berlin) and Tim Neuger (an art expert educated in the United States) were able to make their mark on the world art scene relatively quickly. Neugeriemschneider discovered the artists Franz Ackermann, Tobias Rehberger, and Thaddeus Strode, whose works now hang in international museums and collections.

07 **Style Games** is a network, a kind of virtual game with pieces of information that function like found objects. Wardrobes by famous designers appear on video screens. The World Cup Final between France and Brazil was shown live in the gallery. Now there is a web site, www.stylegames.net, and also a commercial branch, making it possible to buy the latest Matti Braun stool with just a mouse click and a credit card.

09 Better to be a prince among painters than a count among photographers, Lois Renner says. Because of this he calls his works paintings, even though they are more like photos. The small worlds he builds at **Galerie Kuckei + Kuckei** on Linienstrasse are as powerful as full room installations, despite their dimunitive size.

Museums

Museuminsel (Museum Island):

A group of five important state museums. A must if you want to impress people with your education and knowledge of the city.

Altes Museum

J 6 *Bodestrasse 1-3 (Mitte); Lustgarten entrance, Hackescher Markt S-Bahn station; Tel. 20 90 50; Tuesday through Sunday 10 a.m. to 6 p.m., closed Mondays.*

Pergamonmuseum

I 5 *Bodestrasse 1-3 (Mitte) Kupfergraben entrance; Hackescher Markt S-Bahn station; Tel. 20 90 55 55 (recorded information); hours as above.*

Antiksammlung (Antique collection) Altes Museum

J 6 *Bodestrasse 1-3 (Mitte); Lustgarten entrance; Hackescher Markt S-Bahn station; Tel. 20 90 52 01; hours as above.*

—01 Camera Work
E7, Kantstrasse 149; Tel. 31 50 47 93
Tuesday through Friday 11 a.m. to 6 p.m.,
Saturday 11 a.m. to 4 p.m.

—02 Haas & Fuchs
D7, Niebuhrstrasse 5; Tel. 881 88 06
Tuesday through Friday 10 a.m. to 1 p.m.,
3 p.m. to 6 p.m., Saturday 11 a.m. to 2 p.m.

—03 Franck + Schulte
D 7, Mommsenstrasse 56. Tel. 324 00 44
Monday through Friday 11 a.m. to 6 p.m.,
Saturday 11 a.m to 3 p.m.

—04 Schipper und Krome
I 5, Auguststrasse 91, Tel. 28 39 01 39
Tuesday through Friday 12 noon to 6 p.m.,
Saturday 1 p.m.to 5 p.m.

—05 Michel Majerus
D 7,Bergstrasse 14, Tel. 285 83 66
Private, open by appointment only.

—06 Contemporary Fine Arts
J 5, Sophienstrasse 21, Tel. 283 65 80
Tuesday through Saturday 11 a.m. to 6 p.m.

—07 Style Games
D 7, Kurfürstendamm 182/183, Tel. 882 63 01
Tuesday, Thursday 10 a.m. to 10:30 p.m.,
Saturday, Sunday 10 a.m. to 7 p.m.

—08 Neugeriemschneider
J 5, Linienstrasse 155, Tel. 30 87 28 10
Tuesday through Saturday 11 a.m. to 6 p.m.

—09 Kuckei+Kuckei
D 7, Linienstrasse 158, Tel. 883 43 54
Tuesday through Friday 11 a.m. to 6 p.m.,
Saturday 11 a.m. to 5 p.m.

Kulturforum Tiergarten:

Next to the Museuminsel, the Kulturforum is the most important cultural complex in Berlin. It includes the new Gemäldegalerie (Painting Gallery), which was opened in 1998 and includes an unusual collection of old masters, and the Neue Nationalgalerie (New National Gallery), which has a superb collection of twentieth century art. Other parts of the Kulturforum are the Kupferstichkabinett, which features outstanding graphic works, the Staatsbibliothek (State Library) and the Philharmonie.

Neue Nationalgalerie

H 7 *Potsdamer Strasse 50 (Tiergarten); Potsdamer Platz subway and S-Bahn station; Tel. 26 66; Tuesday through Friday*

Vigil at the Wall: Checkpoint Charlie

In a glass house: Neue Nationalgalerie

10 a.m. to 6 p.m., Saturday, Sunday 11 a.m. to 6 p.m.

Gemäldegalerie

H 7 *Matthäikirchplatz 8 (Tiergarten); Potsdamer Platz subway and S-Bahn station; Tel. 266 29 51; Tuesday through Sunday 10 a.m. to 6 p.m.*

Kupferstichkabinett

H 7 *Matthäikirchplatz 6 (Tiergarten); Potsdamer Platz subway and S-Bahn station; Tel. 266 20 23; hours as above.*

Haus am Checkpoint Charlie/ Mauermuseum

I 7 *Friedrichstrasse 43/44 (Kreuzberg); Kochstrasse subway station; Tel. 253 72 50; daily 9 a.m. to 10 p.m.*

Permanent exhibitions with an emphasis on history. Themes: the Wall, Berlin as a city on the front of the Cold War, and human rights.

Sammlung Berggruen

C 6 *In Western Stülerbau, Schlossstrasse 1 (Charlottenburg); Sophie-Charlotte-Platz subway station; Tel. 326 95 80; Tuesday through Friday 10 a.m. to 6 p.m., Saturday, Sunday 11 a.m. to 6 p.m.*

Internationally renowned gallery owner Heinz Berggruen displays his extensive

collection in a permanent exhibition, including works by Picasso and Paul Klee.

Deutsches Technikmuseum Berlin

H 8 *Trebbiner Strasse 7-9 (Kreuzberg); Gleisdreieck subway station; Tel. 25 48 40; Tuesday through Friday 9 a.m. to 5:30 p.m., Saturday, Sunday 10 a.m. to 6 p.m.*

Exhibitions from about 100 collections and museums that existed in Berlin before 1945, for example the Postal Museum, the Transport and Building Museum, and a large collection about air travel.

Anything like New York? Kulturforum Tiergarten

Deutsche Guggenheim Berlin

I 6 *Unter den Linden 13-15 (Mitte); Französische Strasse subway station; Tel. 20 20 93-0/11; daily 11 a.m. to 8 p.m.*

A joint venture of the Solomon R. Guggenheim Foundation and Deutsche Bank. Three to four exhibitions a year, which are organized by both parties. Also spectacular new acquisitions by Deutsche Bank.

Guggenheim: Lots of light

Käthe-Kollwitz-Museum Berlin

E 8 *Fasanenstrasse 24 (Charlottenburg); Uhlandstrasse subway station; Tel. 882 52 10; Wednesday through Monday 11 a.m. to 6 p.m., closed Tuesdays.*

Collection of the late gallery owner Pels-Leusden provides an overview of the work of Käthe Kollwitz.

Jüdisches Museum (Jewish Museum)

J 7 *Libeskind-Bau, Lindenstrasse 9-14 (Kreuzberg); Hallesches Tor subway station; Tel. 25 99 34 10;*

Exhibitions will begin in October 2000, but tours of the building can be booked by telephone.

Werkbundarchiv

I 7 *Martin-Gropius-Bau, Stresemannstrasse 110 (Kreuzberg); Anhalter Bahnhof S-Bahn station; Tel. 25 48 60; daily 10 a.m. to 8 p.m.*

An impressive archive of industrial design. Will be opened at its new location in the Martin-Gropius-Bau in June 1999.

Asian Fine Arts Factory

J 5 *Sophienstrasse 18 (Mitte); Hackescher Markt S-Bahn station; Tel. 28 39 13 87; Tuesday through Saturday 12 a.m. to 7 p.m.*

Contemporary Asian art. Features artists like Ik-Joong Kang, Xu Bing, and Tsuyshi Ozawa.

Galerie Eigen+Art

J 5 *Auguststrasse 26 (Mitte); Oranienburger Strasse S-Bahn station; Tel. 280 66 05; Tuesday through Friday 2 p.m. to 7 p.m., Saturday 11 a.m. to 5 p.m.*

International and contemporary artists. Works by Olaf Nicolai, Carsten Nicolai and Fabrice Hubert.

Green light for late-night viewing

Galerie Max Hetzler

I 7 *Zimmerstrasse 89 (Kreuzberg); Kochstrasse subway station; Tel. 229 24 37; Tuesday through Saturday 11 a.m. to 6 p.m.*

Classics of American and German art from the '80s and '90s: Jeff Koons, Martin Kippenberger and Gerhard Merz.

Mehdi Chouakri

J 5 *Gipsstrasse 11 (Mitte); Hackescher Markt S-Bahn station; Tel. 28 39 11 53; Monday through Friday 2 p.m. to 7 p.m., Saturday 1 p.m. to 7 p.m.*

A mixture of established artists like John Armleder, Sylvie Fleury, and Gerwald Rockenschaub and younger talents like Monika Bonvicini and Isabel Hamerdinger.

Deutsches Theater

H 5 *Schumannstrasse 13a (Mitte); Friedrichstrasse subway and S-Bahn station; Tel. 28 44 12 22; box office: Monday through Saturday 11 a.m. to 7:30 p.m., Sunday 3 p.m. to 7:30 p.m.; Amex, Diners, Euro, Visa.*

Probably the most renowned among Berlin's many and varied theaters. Home of Max Reinhardt's theatrical empire.

Maxim Gorki

I 6 *Am Festungsgraben 1 (Mitte); Friedrichstrasse subway and S-Bahn station; Tel. 20 22 10; box office: Monday through*

Saturday 1 p.m. to 6:30 p.m., Sunday 3 p.m. to 6:30 p.m.; Amex, Visa, Euro.

The theater of actors and storytellers. The latest sensation was Der Hauptmann von Köpenick with the famous and multitalented Katharina Thalbach directing (and substituting in the title role).

Great artists in residence: Hirst and Wilson at DAAD Galerie

Renaissance Theater

E 7 Hardenbergstrasse 6 (Charlottenburg); Ernst-Reuter-Platz subway station; Tel. 312 42 02; box office: Monday through Friday 10:30 a.m. to 7 p.m.; Amex, Euro, Visa.

The best place for suspenseful, entertaining (i.e. popular) theater in Berlin.

Theater & Komödie am Ku'damm

E 7 Kurfürstendamm 206-209 (Charlottenburg) Uhlandstrasse subway station; Tel. 885 91 10; box office: Monday through Saturday 10 a.m. to 8 p.m., Sunday 2 p.m. to 8 p.m.; Visa, Euro, Amex.

An ideal place to see popular comedies and favorite-son stars with considerable mileage on the boards, like Harald Juhnke and Loriot.

Berliner Ensemble

I 5 Bertold-Brecht-Platz 1 (Mitte); Friedrichstrasse subway and S-Bahn station; Tel. 282 31 60, 28 40 80; www.berliner-ensemble.de; box office: Monday through Saturday 11 a.m. to 6 p.m., Sunday 3 p.m. to 6 p.m. (also open on the evening of the performance); Visa, Euro, Amex.

You can almost feel the ghosts of the great playwrights and directors Bertolt Brecht and Heiner Müller

Hamburger Bahnhof

Right next to the Lehrter Stadtbahnhof, which is going to become a giant transportation center, a new cultural enterprise is gathering steam.

At least since the Musée d'Orsay was created in Paris, people have been turning old train stations into museums. It's the same in Berlin: the first train from Hamburg arrived at Hamburger Bahnhof on December 12, 1846. On Novermber 1, 1996 the former train station opened its doors as a museum of contemporary life, and quickly became a major force in the Berlin art world. Behind the severe, eggshell-colored façade of the main building lies the main hall, which resembles the inside of a church. Two wings and the east gallery also offer space for exhibitions. Most of these come from the collection of Erich Marx, which is dominated by the works of Beuys, Kiefer, Rauschenberg and Warhol.

H 5 Hamburger Bahnhof, Museum für Gegenwart Invalidenstrasse 50/51, Tel. 397 83 40 Tuesday through Friday 10 a.m. to 6 p.m., Saturday, Sunday 11 a.m. to 6 p.m., closed Mondays Entry: DM 12

Plenty of space for art: Hamburger Bahnhof

Museums on the edge

Stasi-Museum
Lichtenberg *Ruschestrasse 103, Haus 1; Magdalenenstrasse subway station; Tel. 553 68 54; Tuesday through Friday 11 a.m. to 6 p.m., Saturday, Sunday 2 p.m. to 6 p.m.*

Ten years after the fall of the Berlin Wall the history of the former East German is still within reach at this museum of the Ruschestrasse.

Hanfmuseum (Hemp Museum)
J 6 *Mühlendamm 5 Alexanderplatz subway and S-bahn station, Tel. 242 48 27 ; Tuesday through Friday 10 a.m. to 8 p.m., Saturday, Sunday 12 p.m. to 8 p.m. Entry: DM 5. DM 3.50 each for groups of six or more*

Not just for stoners, the museum explains all the different uses for hemp.

Teddy-Museum
D 8 *Kurfürstendamm 147 Adenauerplatz subway station; Tel. 893 39 65; Wednesday through Friday 3 p.m. to 6 p.m., Saturday, Sunday 12 p.m. to 8 p.m. Entry: Donation*

An impressive collection in a private 4th floor apartment.

Schwules Museum (Gay Museum)
I 8 *Mehringdamm 61; Mehringdamm subway station; Tel. 693 11 72; Wednesday through Sunday 2 p.m. to 6 p.m., Thursdays to 9 p.m.*

A milestone of Berlin's gay movement and the best museum of its kind in the world.

when you visit this theater (both once served as former directors). The glowing red letters of the name are visible from far off.

Volksbühne
K 5 *Rosa-Luxemburg-Platz (Mitte); R.-Luxemburg-Platz subway station; Tel. 24 06 55; box office: daily 12 noon to 6 p.m. and evening of the performance; no credit cards.*

The last great political theater in Berlin, Volksbühne is located between Kreuzberg and Prenzlauer Berg, and too radical to easily classify.

Kammerspiele
F 5 *Alt-Moabit 98 (Tiergarten); Turmstrasse subway station; Tel. 391 55 43; box office: Monday through Sunday noon to 6 p.m.*

An institution among venues for children and young people, featuring classic stories like The Jungle Book.

Carrousel Theater an der Parkaue
Lichtenberg Parkaue 29; Frankfurter Allee subway and S-Bahn station; Tel. 55 77 52 52/53; box office: Monday through Friday 10 a.m. to 5 p.m.; no credit cards.

Germany's biggest theater for young people.

Schaubühne am Lehniner Platz
D 8 *Kurfürstendamm 153 (Wilmersdorf); Adenauerplatz subway station; Tel. 89 00 23; Box office: Monday*

through Saturday 11 a,m. to 6:30 p.m., Sunday 3 p.m. to 6:30 p.m., and evening of performance; Amex, Visa, Euro.

Located in the Universum-Kino, which is now an official cultural monument. Shows plays by writers like Botho Strauss and Anton Chekov under the direction of Thomas Ostermeier, formerly of the celebrated Baracke Theater (below).

Schaubühne: A memorial to Anton Chekov

Baracke
H 5 *Schumannstrasse 13a (Mitte); Friedrichstrasse subway and S-Bahn station; Tel. 28 44 12 22; box office: Monday through Saturday 11 a.m. to 6:30 p.m. at Deutsches Theater, evening of performance; no credit cards.*

This theater has attained cult status with plays like Shopping and Fucking, and plans to continue the wildcard tradition under its new management.

Hackesches Hoftheater
J 5 *Rosenthaler Strasse 40 (Mitte); Hackescher Markt S-Bahn station; Tel. 283 25 87; no credit cards.*

The ground floor of the Hackesche Höfe features musical and literary theater, and sometimes even gestural theater. Also hosts concerts of Yiddish music.

Grips Theater

F 6 *Altonaer Strasse 22/ Hansaplatz (Tiergarten); Hansaplatz subway station; Tel. 391 40 04; tickets in advance: Monday through Friday 12 noon to 6 p.m., Saturday, Sunday 11 a.m. to 5 p.m.; no credit cards.*

A renowned theater for children, young people, and adults who demand realism and boast elevated moral standards.

Friends of Italian Opera

I 9 *Fidicinstrasse 40 (Kreuzberg); Platz der Luftbrücke subway station; Tel. 691 12 11; tickets on evening of performance from 6:30 p.m.; no credit cards.*

Theater for international groups and performances. Named for the group of mafiosi characters in the Billy Wilder film Some Like it Hot.

Ufa Fabrik

Tempelhof Viktoriastrasse 10-18; Ullsteinstrasse subway station; Tel. 75 50 30; no credit cards.

Place for education and performances featuring a children's circus, cabaret, variety theater, and jazz.

Musicals

Theater des Westens

E 7 *Kantstrasse 12 (Charlottenburg); Zoo subway and S-Bahn station; Tel. 882 28 88; box office: Tuesday through Saturday 11 a.m. to 7 p.m., Sunday 2 p.m.–5 p.m.; Visa, Euro.*

Magnificent façade, magnificent productions, magnificent stars, including divas Ute Lemper, Helen Schneider, and Hildegard Knef.

Friedrichstadtpalast

I 5 *Friedrichstrasse 107 (Mitte); Friedrichstrasse subway and S-Bahn station; Tel. 232 62 474; box office: Monday 10 a.m. to 6 p.m., Tuesday through Sunday 1 p.m. to 7 p.m., evening of performance; Amex, Visa, Euro.*

The legend lives on, along with the style of the '20s. The new revue is called Elements, and shows the ensemble in tip-top form.

Der Herr der Ringe im Fantasy-Zelt (The Lord of the Rings in the Fantasy Tent)

I 5 *Oranienburger Strasse 58 (Mitte); Oranienburger Tor subway station; ticket hotline 0180/530 20 25; www.herr-der-ringe.de; Amex, Visa, Euro, Diners.*

J. R. R. Tolkein's famous trilogy hits the stage in a fantastic, dreamlike tent on Oranienburger Strasse.

See you next Sunday

There is a dancing boom in Berlin: cha-cha-cha, foxtrot, and Viennese waltzes are all the rage. It's not a fad from America or a cult film that everyone is trying to imitate—it just started somehow. And for some reason more and more people are out there learning the steps. Dance schools are getting fuller, the universities are offering classes, and the gay and lesbian subculture also seems to have caught the bug. There are classes for every rhythm: Argentine tango, salsa, merengue and—the current trend— swing.

SO 36
K 7 *Oranienstrasse 190; Sundays from 7 p.m.*

Tanzschule bebop
J 8 *Mehringdamm 33; Sundays from 7 p.m.*

Walzerlinksgestrickt
I 8 *Am Tempelhofer Berg 7d Sundays from 6 p.m., Wednesdays from 8:30 p.m.*

Alte TU-Mensa (Old cafeteria at the TU student dining hall)
E 7 *Hardenbergstrasse 12; Tuesdays from 8 p.m.*

Home of big concepts: Komische Oper

Progress has a tradition. In accordance with this motto, every performance here shows a need to come to terms with the present. Drama and music become unified in a single concept.

Tickets in advance

Hekticket Theaterkasse

E 7 *Hardenbergstrasse 29a (Charlottenburg); Zoo subway and S-Bahn station; Tel. 230 99 30; www.berlinonline.de/hekticket Monday through Friday 9 a.m. to 8 p.m., Saturday 10 a.m. to 8 p.m., Sunday 4 p.m. to 8 p.m.; no credit cards.*

Beginning at 3 p.m., theater tickets for performances on the same day are sold at a reduced price.

Berliner Theater und Konzertkassen (Berlin Theater and Concert Box Offices)

J 6 *Spreeufer 6 (Mitte); Alexanderplatz S-Bahn station; Tel. 241 46 35; Fax 241 43 82; Monday through Friday 10 a.m. to 6 p.m., Saturday until 2 p.m.; no credit cards.*

Has other branches in the Kaufhof department store at Alexanderplatz and the Kaufhof at Hauptbahnhof.

KOKA 36

K 8 *Oranienstrasse 29 (Kreuzberg); Kottbusser Damm subway station; Tel. 615 88 18; www.*

Staatsoper Unter den Linden

I 6 *Unter den Linden 7 (Mitte); Friedrichstrasse S-Bahn station; Tel. 203 545 55; box office: Monday through Friday 10 a.m. to 6 p.m., Saturday, Sunday 2 p.m. to 6 p.m.; Euro, Visa, Amex.*

Has the longest tradition among Berlin's opera houses, and seats about 1,400 spectators.

Deutsche Oper

D 6 *Bismarckstrasse 35 (Charlottenburg) Deutsche Oper subway station; Tel. 343 84 01; tickets in advance: Monday through Saturday from one to eleven hours before the beginning of the performance, Sunday 10 a.m. to 2 p.m.; Euro, Visa, Amex.*

Berlin's newest opera house places functionality before many other concerns. It often features works by Wagner, Verdi, or Mozart.

Komische Oper

I 6 *Behrenstrasse 55-57 (Mitte); Friedrichstrasse S-Bahn station; Tel. 47 99 74 00; box office (Unter den Linden 41): Monday through Saturday 11 a.m. to 7 p.m., Sunday from 1 p.m., evening of performance; Visa, Amex, Diners, Euro.*

icf.de/koka36; Monday through Friday 9 a.m. to 7 p.m., Saturday 10 a.m. to 2 p.m.; no credit cards.

Tickets for all Alba (basketball), Capitals (ice hockey) and Eisbären (ice hockey) home games.

Cinemas

Cinemaxx

K 3 *Foxstrasse 5 (Tiergarten); Potsdamer Platz subway and S-Bahn station; Tel. 44 31 63 16; no credit cards.*

An enormous theater complex with nineteen screens and 3,500 seats. Still, on the weekend this usually isn't enough. Good points: the latest technology and lots of legroom. Bad point: the foyer is a little too small.

Imax

H 7 *Marlene-Dietrich-Platz 4 (Tiergarten); Potsdamer Platz subway and S-Bahn station; Tel. 44 31 61 31; www.imax-berlin.de.*

Gigantic spectacle in 3-D. The screen has an area of 540 square meters. Shows good documentaries.

Imax: new dimensions in Potsdamer Platz

Cinemaxx Colosseum

K 3 *Schönhauser Allee 123 (Prenzlauer Berg); Schönhauser Allee subway and S-Bahn station; Tel. 44 31 63 16.*

The second Cinemaxx, located in what used to be East Berlin. Same brilliant technology and comfortable seats as the other Cinemaxx, but with a much more spacious foyer.

Zoo Palast

E 7 *Hardenbergstrasse 29a (Charlottenburg); Zoo subway and S-Bahn station; Tel. 25 41 47 77; no credit cards.*

This used to be the cinema for premieres at the Berlinale (Berlin Film Festival), but now, after forty-two years at Zoo, the main shows are moving east to Potsdamer Platz. The cinema has nine auditoriums, and the first one is enormous.

Astor

E 7 *Kurfürstendamm 217 (Charlottenburg); Uhlandstrasse subway station; Tel. 881 11 08; no credit cards.*

A peaceful theater with soft armchairs. Films for more discerning viewers.

Delphi

E 7 *Kantstrassse 12a (Charlottenburg); Zoo subway and S-Bahn station; Tel. 312 10 26; no credit cards.*

The Delphi still embodies the charm of the first years of West Berlin with its columns, its entryway, and its large front foyer.

Arsenal

F 8 *Welserstrasse 25 (Schöneberg); Wittenbergplatz subway station; Tel. 219 00 10; no credit cards.*

High-quality, unusual films, all outside the mainstream. Interesting programming, and definitely worth a look.

Life after the Berlinale?: Zoo Palast

International

K 6 *Karl-Marx-Allee 33 (Mitte); Schillingstrasse subway station; Tel. 24 75 60 11; no credit cards.*

Back in the days of the GDR, this was the big cinema for premieres. Now it has a cult success with the film Honecker-Lounge.

Filmtheater in den Hackeschen Höfen

J 5 *Rosenthaler Strasse 40/41(Mitte); Hackescher Markt S-Bahn station Tel. 283 46 03 No credit cards.*

Four screens that show exclusively non-Hollywood fare. After a cine-date, the nearby Zeobar deserves a visit.

Kurbel

D 8 *Giesebrechtstrasse 4 (Charlottenburg); Savignyplatz S-Bahn station; Tel. 883 53 25; no credit cards.*

Back in the early '70s the Kurbel was an X-rated theater, and it wasn't until 1974 that films with plots started to show up on the screen. Sneak preview showings in the original language are a specialty of the house.

Philharmonie

H 7 *Herbert-von-Karajan-Strasse 1 (Tiergarten); Potsdamer Platz subway and S-Bahn station; Tel. 25 48 80; box office: Monday through Friday 3 p.m. to 6 p.m., Saturday, Sunday 11 a.m. to 2 p.m.; Amex, Visa, Euro.*

One of the best orchestras in the world. Because of its asymmetical, tentlike roof, the building has been called "Circus Karajan."

Konzerthaus Berlin

I 6 *Gendarmenmarkt (Mitte); Französische Strasse subway station; Tel. 203 09 21 01/02; box office: Monday through Saturday 12 noon to 6 p.m. Sunday 12 noon to 4 p.m.; Amex, Visa, Euro.*

Architecturally, this building on the Gendarmenmarkt is stunning. Permanent home of the Berliner Sinfonieorchester (Berlin Symphony Orchestra).

PHOTOS: Jörg Lehmann (3)

Basket-Boom

Prenzlauer Berg is the home of basketball in Germany, thanks to the Albatrosses.

It's crunch time at Max-Schmelling-Hall. People are chanting "Defense, Defense." Seven thousand pairs of eyes stare at the orange ball, which has landed in the wrong hands. Then suddenly every-one is silent. The ball flies in a high arc toward the basket—the wrong one. Then a cry of relief, because two hands—the right ones—have caught the ball. Henrik Rödl of Alba Berlin stuffs the ball in the hoop at the other end of the court, the spectators rise from their seats, and the building foundations shake.

The days when "Did you see the game yesterday?" always referred to soccer are over, at least in Berlin. Since the Alba team took up residence in Prenzlauer Berg, right in the

Where can I play streetball?

Kreuzberg
Statthaus
Böcklerpark
Prinzenstrasse

Yaam
new location not yet known

Schöneberg
Nike Urban Jungle Court
Kufsteiner Strasse/
Mettestrasse

Wannsee
Dreilindenschule
Dreilindenstrasse

Zehlendorf
Gesamtschule
In Hegewinkel

Sport und Vereinszentrum
Marshallstrasse 3

Neukölln
Hasenheide
Columbiadamm

Mitte
Nike Regrind Court
Alexanderplatz

Spandau
Hakenfelde Stadium
Hakenfelder Strasse

Hohenschönhausen
2. Gesamtschule
Sandinostrasse 10

Coach Svetislav Pesic giving a motivational speech

city's social center, the sports has abandoned the marginal status that it still has in many German cities.

Few teams in the German Football League attract more spectators, and the average attendance figures at an Alba game can be compared with those of teams in countries like Italy, Spain, or

Nike's booklet on streetball, along with a list of places to play, is available here: Nike, Hessenring 13a, 64546 Mörfelden.

When seconds feel like hours: Alba fans

Greece, where basketball is much more popular.

In 1996, most people thought team manager Marco Baldi was crazy when he moved Alba from Charlottenburg's Sömmeringhalle, which seats 2,500, to Max-Schmelling-Halle, which seats 8,000. But the changeover has proved to be a stroke of genius: the new venue is more comfortable than the old and has a jazzier atmosphere. Also, the move coincided with the team's soaring success. But the improved conditions at the new facility and the greater capacity for spectators, combined with the team's success, have created a much bigger group of Alba fans, proving that Baldi knew exactly what he was doing. *Matti Lieske*

Alba ticket hotline Tel. 53 43 80 00, daily from 6 a.m. to 12 p.m. Prices: German league DM 11.25 – DM 41.25; European league DM 21.25 – DM 101.25. Internet: www.albaberlin.de.

Fitness centers

Jopp Frauen Fitness
F 7 *Tauentzienstrasse 13 (Charlottenburg); Kurfürstendamm subway station; Tel. 21 01 11; Monday through Friday 7 a.m. to 11 p.m., Saturday, Sunday 10 a.m. to 8 p.m.; no credit cards; One-day pass: DM 35.*
Everything in women's fitness: jazz dancing, ski gymnastics, weight machines, and more. Also offers child care. Large sauna for relaxation.

Ars Vitalis Fitnessclub
G 9 *Hauptstrasse 19 (Schöneberg); Kleistpark subway station; Tel. 788 35 63; Monday through Friday 10 a.m. to 11:30 p.m., Saturday, Sunday 11 a.m. to 9 p.m.; no credit cards; one-day pass: DM 45.*

Calves of steel: Ars Vitalis

Working out at Healthland

A modern, tastefully arranged fitness center. Offers aerobic gymnastics, weight machines, and cardiovascular training. When you're done with your workout, you can sweat some more in the sauna or go for a refreshing swim in the pool.

Healthland

I 6 *Behrenstrasse 48 (Mitte); Französische Strasse subway station; Tel. 20 63 53 00; Monday through Friday 6 a.m. to 11 p.m., Saturday, Sunday 10 a.m. to 10 p.m.; no credit cards; one-day pass: DM 50.*

First-class services for people who want to stay in shape: cardiovascular training, fitness and strength workouts, and spinning classes, the new trend from across the Atlantic. Personal trainers also available.

Dörbrandt Fitness

D 8 *Kurfürstendamm 182/183 (Charlottenburg); Adenauerplatz subway station; Tel. 882 63 01; Monday, Wednesday, Friday 7 a.m. to 10:30 p.m., Tuesday, Thursday 10 a.m. to 10:30 p.m., Saturday, Sunday 10 a.m. to 7 p.m.; no credit cards; one-day pass: DM 29, ten day pass: DM 245.*

A favorite of the Charlottenburg crowd after a hard day at the office. An extensive fitness program with cardiovascular training, aerobics, and yoga.

Life Sport + Art Villa Wiegand

A 9 *Bismarckallee 44 (Grunewald), Bus 119; Tel. 825 30 68; Monday, Wednesday, Thursday 9 a.m. to 10 p.m. Tuesday, Friday 8 a.m. to 10 p.m., Saturday 9 a.m. to 7 p.m.; no credit cards.*

Fitness center for well-heeled Grunewalders. Extremely competent trainers put doctors, lawyers, and actors through their paces. Very comprehensive fitness program, with jogging in the park during the summer.

Racket paradise: Tennis & Squash City

J.J. Men Fitness

D 7 *Wilmersdorfer Strasse 82-83 (Charlottenburg); Adenauerplatz subway station; Tel. 324 10 25; Monday, Wednesday, Friday 10 a.m. to 11 p.m., Tuesday, Thursday 7 a.m. to 11 p.m., Saturday, Sunday 10 a.m. to 6 p.m.; One-day pass: DM 20.*

Berlin's only centrally located men's fitness center. Offers cardiofitness, sauna, solarium, and a rehab program for sports-related injuries.

Tennis

TCW Tenniscenter Weissensee

M 1 *Roelckestrasse 106 (Weissensee); Pasedagplatz tram stop; Tel. 927 45 94; Monday through Friday 7 a.m. to 12 p.m., Saturday, Sunday 8 a.m. to 12 p.m.*

Eight tennis courts. An hour with a trainer costs DM 45. Badminton courts, well-lit halls, tennis school, table tennis, sauna, food, summer terrace, sporting goods shop. Full of East Berlin charm.

Tennis & Squash City

D 8 *Brandenburgische Strasse 53 (Wilmersdorf); Konstanzer Strasse subway station; Tel. 873 90 97; Monday through Friday 8 a.m. to 10 p.m., Saturday, Sunday 7 a.m. to 12 p.m. no credit cards; tennis courts Monday through Friday DM 17 - DM 33.*

An hour with a trainer costs DM 50. Pleasant, friendly atmosphere. In addition to tennis, squash, and badminton, there is also a driving range for golf.

Alpha Tennis
Gross-Ziethen Karl-Marx-Strasse/Querweg; Tel. 03379/44 45 70; daily 8 a.m. to 11 p.m.; no credit cards; about 30 minutes outside Berlin.

The trip out to the countryside is worth it: well-tended courts for an elegant game of tennis.

Squash artists: Fit Fun

Squash

Fit Fun
E 7 Uhlandstrasse 194 (Charlottenburg); Zoo subway and S-Bahn station; Tel. 312 50 82; daily 8 a.m. to 12 p.m.; Visa, Euro; from DM 20, from DM 16 for students.

Centrally located, with thirteen squash courts

on two floors. Popular among students. Also has a bar where you can drink a protein shake and maybe strike up a conversation with a well-muscled someone.

Sport Oase
F 5 Stromstrasse 11-17 (Tiergarten); Turmstrasse subway station; Tel. 394 50 94 daily 8 a.m. to 11 p.m.; courts cost DM 15 in the morning, DM 20 in the afternoon or evening.

Squash balls and badminton feathers fly through the air. Simple facilities and affordable prices draw a young crowd.

Bicycle rental

Fahrradstation
J 5 Rosenthaler Strasse 40-41 (Mitte); Hackescher Markt subway station; Tel. 28 38 48 48; Monday through Friday 10 a.m. to 7 p.m., Saturday 10 a.m. to 4 p.m., Sundays only at the train-stations; no credit cards; prices from DM 20 per day.

Also rents bikes at the Zoo and Lichtenberg train stations. Rickshaws too. The Fahrradstation offers tours of Berlin and Brandenburg.

Fahrradvermietung am Europa-Center
F 7 Europa-Center im 15. OG (Charlottenburg); Wittenbergplatz subway station; Tel. 261 20 94, 261 20 01; April through October daily 9 a.m. to 8 p.m.; no credit cards;

Mike's & Billie's: Keep on rollin' in the free world

rental: DM 20 per day. Sturdy bikes that are well-suited to the demands of Berlin's streets.

Skating

Skating Verleih
Ski-Shop Charlottenburg C 6 Otto-Suhr-Allee 115 (Charlottenburg); Richard-Wagner-Platz subway station; Tel. 341 48 70; Monday through Friday 10 a.m. to 7 p.m., Saturday 10 a.m. to 4 p.m.; no credit cards; inline skate rental: Friday through Monday DM 35 per day, otherwise DM 15.

Everything for nimble feet—skis, snowboards, inline skates for sale or rent.

Mike's & Billie's
G 8 Motzstrasse 9 (Schöneberg); Nollendorfplatz subway station; Tel. 215 70 70; Friday through Monday 11 a.m. to 7:30 p.m., Saturday 10:30 a.m. to 4

p.m.; no credit cards; inline skate rental: Friday through Monday DM 30 per day, otherwise DM 20.

A trendy shop for sportswear and fashionable brands. Helpful salespeople.

Skating routes

Winterfeldtplatz
G 8 *(Schöneberg); Nollendorfplatz subway station.*

Everything on eight wheels, from beginners with bloody knees to total skating fanatics. There is usually a hockey game going on, too, for contenders.

Kronprinzessinnen-weg
Zehlendorf; Nikolassee S-Bahn station.

A straight path in the middle of the forest, parallel to the highway. If you make it all the way to Wannsee, there are plenty of restaurants and bars where you can recharge your batteries.

Strasse des 17. Juni
E-H 6 *(Tiergarten); Unter den Linden S-Bahn station*

Skaters and bicyclists dash from the Brandenburger Tor to the Siegessäule. The meadows in the Tiergarten offer a comfortable place for a rest, and at Charlottenburger Tor there is a big antique and flea market every weekend.

Sportforum Hohenschönhausen
Konrad-Wolf-Strasse; ticket hotline Tel. 53 43 50 00; tickets from DM 25 (reduced price DM 20), children DM 15.

Jogging

F-H 6 ### Tiergarten
This green oasis is an ideal place for jogging. Afterwards you can go for an apple juice with

The Polar Bears are on the loose

If you go into the Wellblechpalast when there's a game, you'll think you've been transported back to the old days when the GDR was alive and well. Fans of the Berlin hockey team the Polar Bears (Eisbären) like to hear socialist songs, like the old hit "Bau auf." Most of the players on the team are from Canada or Scandinavia, and need to be reminded that songs like "Dy-na-mo" are about them—the team changed its name from Dynamo in 1992. In the days of the GDR Dynamo was one of only two hockey teams, and the whipping boy of the German league. But then someone had an idea: an international team that plays good hockey—and it worked: third place in 1997, second place in 1998. This year the team made it into the final four in the European Cup. Five thousand spectators, including skinheads, lefties, and "normal" people, now show up regularly to cheer the Polar Bears on. Their favorite opponents are the Capitals, a local rival from the western part of the city. Even though some of the chants have a warlike tone, fans depart peacefully after the games. Join them—the Polar Bears are cool!

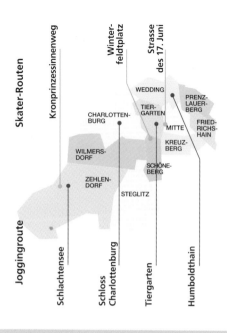

Skater-Routen · Kronprinzessinnenweg · Winterfeldtplatz · Strasse des 17. Juni

WEDDING · PRENZLAUER-BERG · CHARLOTTENBURG · TIERGARTEN · FRIEDRICHSHAIN · MITTE · WILMERSDORF · KREUZBERG · ZEHLENDORF · SCHÖNEBERG · STEGLITZ

Joggingroute · Schlachtensee · Schloss Charlottenburg · Tiergarten · Humboldthain

mineral water at Café am neuen See, the hippest beer garden in Berlin.

L 5 Schloss Charlottenburg

In the imposing castle gardens it is sometimes hard to decide if you should run or stop to admire the scenery. Good for beginners, because you have to run all around the grounds before it adds up to a few kilometers.

Zehlendorf Schlachtensee

The path around the lake is about five

Hertha's Heartbreakers

Berlin's football clubs are waking up, and people starting to take notice

Tennis Borussia
2. Bundesliga
(Second German League)

Stadium: Mommsenstadion, Waldschulallee 34-42 in Charlottenburg.

Tickets: Tel. 306 96 10.

Entry: seats from DM 30, standing from DM 15, reduced price DM 10, children DM 5, family ticket DM 30.

Successes: 1998 German Amateur Champions, twelve times Berlin champions and cup winners.

Stars: The only real one is on the trainer's bench: Winnie Schäfer.

Image: The team is on the road to success, and no one seems to care. This multicultural team plays good football, but they have not yet been able to win the hearts of fans.

1. FC Union Berlin
Regional League
North-East

Stadium: At the Alte Försterei, at the Wuhlheide in Köpenick

Tickets: Tel. 656 68 80.

Entry: seats DM 20, reduced price DM 15, standing DM 10, reduced price DM 8, children DM 4.

Successes: Free German Federation of Trade Unions Cup 1968.

Stars: Peter Közle, a midfielder, and goalkeeper Oskar Kosche, a crowd favorite.

Image: Underdog in the days of the separate Germanys– tolerated from above, admired from below. Battle cry: "Iron, Union!" Goal: To become the number two team in Berlin.

Pool players show their stuff

kilometers long. An ideal run, with the trees reflecting beautifully in the water. Tired legs can take a swim in the lake afterward to cool off.

I 3 Humboldthain

A platform affords an excellent view of the park. It's about fifty steps—a brilliant workout. The path around the park is about three kilometers long. If you're training

for a triathlon, you'll appreciate the outdoor pool next door where you can swim a few laps.

Billardair

H 9 *Monumentenstrasse 35 (Schöneberg); Kleistpark subway station; Tel. 784 11 77; Monday through Friday from 4 p.m., Saturday, Sunday from 2 p.m.; no credit cards.*
Salon with pool, snooker, and carambol tables. Friendly pub atmosphere.

Pool

K 4 *Immanuelkirchstrasse 14 (Prenzlauer Berg); Senefelder Platz subway station; Tel. 442 82 70; 24 hours daily; no credit cards; Monday through Friday 6 a.m. to 6 p.m. DM 6, 6 p.m. to 12 p.m. DM 12.90, 12 p.m. to 6 p.m. DM 10, Saturday, Sunday DM 12.90.*

A popular meeting place among young people from the neighborhood, especially in the evenings. Serious pool hall atmosphere with forty-one tables.

Billard International

E 7 *Knesebeckstrasse 38-49*

Hertha BSC Berlin 1. Bundesliga (First German League)
Stadium: Olympiastadion.
Tickets: Tel. 01805/43 78 42.
Entry: from DM 12, seats only.
Successes: German Champion in 1930 and 1931.
Stars: Strikers Michael Preetz and Dariusz Wosz, former players on the German national team.
Image: Thanks to millions from Ufa—a film company—and team-work by coach Jürgen Röber and manager Dieter Hoeness, Hertha has become one of the top clubs. **Problem:** Some right-wing fans, and the rough crowd is impossible to ignore at a game.

Berliner with a nose for goals. Hertha's Michael Preetz

Environmentally friendly: Berliners take to their skateboards.

(Charlottenburg); Savignyplatz S-Bahn station; Tel. 883 39 12; 24 hours daily; no credit cards. pool, snooker, carambol.

Sometimes it's so quiet the only thing you can hear is the sound of the balls colliding for serious players.

Sauna Bad im BBZ

H7 Lützowstrasse 106 (Tiergarten); Kurfürstenstrasse subway station; Tel. 262 28 27; Monday through Saturday 4 p.m. to 11 p.m.; Monday is women's day; no credit cards; day pass: DM 30.

Berlin's first esoteric sauna with solarium, massage, swimming pool, bio-sauna, and charming garden.

Hamam in der Schokofabrik

K 8 Mariannenstrasse 6 (Kreuzberg); Görlitzer Bahnhof. subway station; Tel. 615 14 64; daily 12 noon to 10 p.m., Monday from 3 p.m.; no credit cards; DM 18 for two and a half hours.

Relaxation for body and soul in a traditional Turkish bath. Women only, please.

Thermen im Europa-Center

F 7 Nürnberger Strasse 7 (Charlottenburg); Ku'damm subway station; Tel. 261 60 31; Monday through Saturday 10 a.m. to 12 p.m., Sunday 10 a.m. to 9 p.m.; no credit cards; day pass DM 35, night rate DM 27.

Dreamy wetlands with indoor and outdoor thermal baths, a geyser, Finnish saunas, Russian steam baths, and more.

Frauensauna (Women's Sauna)

D 8 Eisenzahnstrasse 14 (Charlottenburg); Adenauerplatz subway station; Tel. 892 70 20; Monday through Friday 10 a.m. to 1 p.m., Saturday, Sunday 12 a.m. to 8 p.m.; no credit cards; day pass DM 25.

Relax and enjoy yourself! It should be easy with four saunas, a fitness center, a big swimming pool, aerobics, and a solarium.

Treibhaus Sauna

K 3 Schönhauser Allee 132 (Prenzlauer Berg); Schönhauser Allee subway station; Tel. 448 45 03; Monday through Thursday 3 p.m. to 7 a.m., also open continuously from 3 p.m. Friday to 7 a.m. Monday; no credit cards; DM 23, DM 35 for a cubicle.

Berlin's best gay sauna. Dry sauna, steam sauna, whirlpool, solarium, and a big bar.

Bowling am Studio

B 7 Kaiserdamm 80/81 (Charlottenburg); Kaiserdamm subway station; Tel. 302 70 94; daily 10 a.m. to 12 p.m., longer on Saturday and Sunday; no credit cards; from DM 3.80 per game.

A colorful crowd migrates between the bar and the billiard

Let the good times roll: Bowling is booming in Berlin.

tables. Some of them even try to knock some pins over. Beerily happy atmosphere.

Bowling am Kurfürstendamm

D 8 *Kurfürstendamm 156 (Charlottenburg); Adenauerplatz subway station; Tel. 892 50 30; Monday, Wednesday, Thursday, Sunday 10 a.m. to 1 p.m., Tuesday, Saturday to 4 a.m., Friday to 3 a.m.; no credit cards; games from DM 3.40 to DM 5.80.*

One of Berlin's biggest bowling alleys. Also has pool tables and pinball machines. It's fun to watch the Korean guests, who come here in droves to play their favorite sport.

Sport shops

bannat

E 8 *Lietzenburger Strasse 65 (Wilmersdorf); Kurfürstendamm subway station; Tel. 882 76 01; Monday through Friday 10 a.m. to 8 p.m., Saturday 10 a.m. to 4 p.m.; Amex, Diners, Visa.*

Globetrotters will find everything they need here for a grand tour: expedition equipment, tents, mountain climbing gear, and tropical clothing.

Karstadt Sport

E 7 *Joachimstaler Strasse 5-6 (Charlottenburg); Zoo subway and S-Bahn station; Tel. 88 02 40; Monday through Friday 10 a.m. to 8 p.m., Saturday 9 a.m. to 4 p.m.; Amex, Diners, Euro, Visa.*

Berlin's biggest sporting goods store offers a gigantic, extremely well-stocked assortment of wares.

360°

D 8 *Pariser Strasse 24 (Wilmersdorf); Adenauerplatz subway station; Tel. 883 85 96; Monday through Friday 11 a.m. to 7:30 p.m., Saturday 10 a.m. to 4 p.m.; Visa, Euro, Amex.*

Cool place with trendy sporting goods for surfers, windsurfers, skateboarders, and snowboarders.

Niketown

F 7 *Tauentzienstrasse 7bc (Charlottenburg); Wittenbergplatz subway station; Tel. 250 70; Monday through Friday 10 a.m. to 8 p.m., Saturday 10 a.m. to 4 p.m.; Visa, Diners, Euro, Amex, Master.*

The latest collections with the swoosh—now in Berlin, in an exclusive new shop. If you wear the same clothes as Pete Sampras or Ronaldo, your game will be twice as good.

A Crumbling Monument

Berlin's Olympic Stadium stands for outstanding athletic achievements, but also for a dark time in history. It is completely run down, but it has a magnificent effect when the stands are full. The architect Werner March drew up plans for the arena in 1936, following suggestions from Hitler. Today the stadium is mostly used by Hertha BSC in the German football league. The last renovation took place twenty-five years ago, before the World Cup, but for political reasons no games were ever played here. Now there are plans to modernize the arena and turn it into a stadium with room for about 75,000 spectators. There are loge seating sections, and new places to eat are being added. Construction will cost DM 500 million, and should be completed by 2004.

Tours from 9 a.m. daily; Olympiastadion subway and S-Bahn station.

Prinzenbad

J8 *Gitschiner Strasse 31 (Kreuzberg); entry: DM 6 (reduced rate DM 4); daily from 7 a.m.*

A family swimming pool, and also a hip meeting place among the younger crowd. Good for swimming laps, with two fifty-meter pools.

Olympiabad

Charlottenburg; Olympischer Platz; entry: DM 6 (reduced rate DM 4); daily from 7 a.m.

Ascetics hone their bodies in front of a historical backdrop.

Alte Halle

D6 *Krumme Strasse 10 (Charlottenburg); entry: DM 6 (reduced rate DM 4); Monday 6 a.m. to 9:30 p.m., Tuesday, Thursday through Saturday 6 a.m to 11 p.m., Wednesday 10 a.m. to 1 p.m., Sunday 4 p.m. to 11 p.m.*

One-hundred-year-old art nouveau swimming pool. If you can't find your bathing suit, go during the times when people are allowed to swim naked.

Bad am Spreewaldplatz

L8 *Wiener Strasse 59h (Kreuzberg); Entry from DM 6 (reduced rate DM 4); Monday 2 p.m. to 11 p.m., Tuesday through Saturday 6 a.m. to 11 p.m., Sunday 8 a.m. to 1 p.m.*

Designer swimming pool with artificial waves and a whirlpool.

Strand at Wannsee

Zehlendorf Wannseebadweg 25; entry: DM 6 (reduced rate DM 4); in May daily from 9 a.m., in June daily from 8 a.m.

Sand and sun. Feels just like a real vacation.

Strand at Müggelsee

Köpenick Fürstenwalder Damm 838; entry: DM 6 (reduced rate DM 4); in May daily from 9 a.m., in June daily from 8 a.m.

Great atmosphere, leisure activities, and clean water—all amid beautiful surroundings.

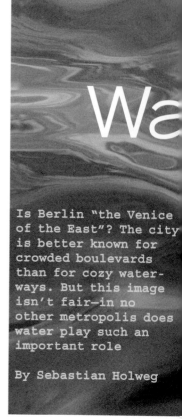

Wa

Is Berlin "the Venice of the East"? The city is better known for crowded boulevards than for cozy waterways. But this image isn't fair—in no other metropolis does water play such an important role

By Sebastian Holweg

Berlin's waterways are both hated and loved. The urban area contains more water than any other in Europe, with 2,600 hectares of lakes and 147 kilometers of rivers and canals. Berlin has many more bridges than Venice, but one scarcely notices them. However, when you ride around beneath them, another world opens up—Berlin as a water city. The waterways are used intensively by both pleasure boaters and professionals. The

ter
Magic

...and if you look closely, you might even see fairies.

PHOTOS: Barbi & Jan (2) Uwe Böhm (1)

working world in conflict with recreation? The state-ordered improvement of the shipping lane from Hanover to Magdeburg to Berlin (Project 17) is meeting massive opposition from people who think the waterways should be reserved for leisure activities.

The Prussian bureaucracy also plays a role in the city's water life. Berlin is the only Bundesland (state) in Germany that requires a separate driver's license for all boat owners, and also has speed limits for boats. The professional boaters could care less. Every year about eleven million metric tons of goods pass through Berlin's one hundred harbors and loading docks. Only Duisburg, Germany's biggest inland port, can top Berlin.

The most economical of all means of transport has a future. The city is making preparations for the next millennium: the Teltow Canal is going to be widened and made deeper. The price: DM 620 million. Beginning in 2010 the canal will be able to accommodate ships of up to two thousand metric tons.

A company offering boat tours has started the new season with new owners and a new idea. The Spreebus, which imitates the Venetian model, is bringing guests to the Nikolaiviertel for the first time. The offices indicate that this is not a shabby operation. There are now eleven moorings in the best part of the city open for water tourists, and the idea of visiting the Museuminsel, the cathedral, and the Nikolaiviertel by water has become a reality. So is Berlin a city that lives on the water. Hardly. Before this happens, Berliners will have to recognize their city's watery side. Tour managers have not been able to muster too much enthusiasm for the city's canals and rivers. But Berlin rivals Venice and Amsterdam in at least one regard: in its abundance of water.

Landmarks

The angel relocated in 1938

Siegessäule
F6 *Grosser Stern/Strasse des 17. Juni; Tiergarten or Bellevue S-Bahn station; viewing platform open from April to October, every day from 9 a.m. to 6 p.m., Mondays from 1 p.m.*

In 1938 Hitler's chief architect, Albert Speer, moved the eight-meter-tall victory statue from its original home in front of the Reichstag to the Tiergarten. The column is sixty-nine meters high and was built in the period between 1865 and 1873

to commemorate the successful Prussian campaigns against France.

Reichstag
H6 *Tiergarten, Platz der Republik*
Built 1884 to 1894 in the style of the Italian High Renaissance, the Reichstag was the seat of parliament during the Wilhelmine era and again during the Weimar Republic. After being set on fire and then bombed during World War II, it was not fully restored until 1970. In 1999, after the government finally completes its move from Bonn, the Reichstag will again be the seat of parliament, with a new dome by prominent architect Norman Foster.

Museuminsel
I5 – J6 *Hackescher Markt S-Bahn station; Tel. 20 90 55 55; Tuesday through Sunday 10 a.m. to 6 p.m.*
In 1841 a royal decree pronounced the island "a district dedicated to art and the study of ancient times." Building began in 1843. Today the Museuminsel is home to all kinds of art treasures, ranging from the ancient to the contemporary.

Schloss Charlottenburg (Charlottenburg Castle)
Charlottenburg Luisenplatz/Spandauer Damm; Bus 109, 145; Tel. 32 09 11; Tuesday through Sunday 10 a.m. to 5 p.m., Thursday until 8 p.m.
During the seventeenth and eighteenth centuries, this building served as a summer residence for the Elector Sophie Charlotte. Today the castle houses a gallery and a museum specializing in the prehistoric and ancient periods.

Gedenkstätte Deutscher Widerstand (Monuments to German Resistance)
G7 *Stauffenbergstrasse 13-14 (Tiergarten); Bus 129; Tel. 26 99 50 00; Monday through Friday 9 a.m. to 6 p.m., Saturday, Sunday 9 a.m. to 1 p.m.*

Lavish grounds: Charlottenburg

Athenian ancestors: Brandenburger Tor

Extensive documentation of resistance to the Nazi regime. Films are shown on the first Sunday of every month, making a valuable contribution to the exhibition.

Brandenburger Tor
H6 *Pariser Platz*
The last of Berlin's fourteen city gates, the Brandenburger Tor was built in the period between 1788 and 1791 by Gotthard Langhans. The model was the propylons in Athens. The gate suffered severe damage during World War II, but was restored in 1957. In 1989 it was transformed from a symbol of Germany's division into a symbol of German reunification.

Kaiser-Wilhelm-Gedächtniskirche
E7 *Breitscheidplatz, Kurfürstendamm subway station or Zoo subway and S-Bahn station; Tel. 218 50 23; church: daily 9 a.m. to 7 p.m.; tower: Monday through Saturday 10 a.m. to 4:30 p.m.*
This neoromantic church was built in 1895

Herford has better air

The best way to get to know a big city is by foot, with certain destinations in mind. Here is a cross section of Berlin, with four tips:

Most people who are looking for nice streets and squares for a leisurely stroll start at Kurfürstendamm, near the centrally located Bahnhof Zoo, and once they get there they stop walking pretty soon. This is probably a mistake, but it's understandable. Many songs have been sung about Kurfürstendamm; it used to be the street that was supposed to embody the spirit of Berlin, and was also a shopping window for the west. These days it resembles a pedestrian zone in a city like Herford (Germany), except that the air in Herford is better. The street is lined with businesses like Gap and McDonald's, which you could find anywhere else in the world, and the buildings seem devoid of all architectural creativity or soul. Cars race down the street, poisoning the air for the sparse trees.

A similar myth exists around Unter den Linden, but unlike the Ku'damm It has a future as one of the new Berlin Republic's most exclusive streets. The beautifully renovated facades—between the Bundestag and Hotel Adlon, the Humboldt University and the Staatsoper— make it clear that this is where power makes its

home. Strips of grass with old-fashioned park benches are a pleasant place to take a stroll. Oranienstrasse represents the historical epoch of the radical neighborhood Kreuzberg in the '70s and '80s. For years anarchists used to do battle with the local police every May 1. Now the area seems depressed. Bars with names like Flammende Herzen (Flaming Hearts) still have their patrons, but the neighborhood seems to be full of old tramps with cans of Schultheiss beer.

Neue Schönhauser Strasse, near the Hackesche Höfe in Mitte, seems well prepared for the leap into the next millennium. The street is only a few hundred meters long, and it doesn't look like much at first sight – the first business is SanAktiv, a favorite meeting place for rehab-types. But just a little bit further on there are many first-class businesses and restaurants. There are many interesting places to investigate, including the cool and exclusive Schwarzenraben" and a gigantic sneaker store.

Multiculturalism and everyday life: Many different cultures and ethnic groups live side by side on Kreuzberg's Oranienstrasse— and most of them have found a home here.

FLEISCH ISCH FLE ISCHI

in memory of Kaiser Friedrich I. Destroyed during a bombing raid in 1943, today the remains of the tower stand as a memorial to the war, with a permanent exhibition within.

Imposing neobaroque

Friedrichswerdersche Kirche

I6 *Werderstrasse 1 (Mitte); Hausvogteiplatz subway station; Tel. 208 13 23; Tuesday through Sunday 10 a.m. to 6 p.m.*

A neogothic brick building, built between 1824 and 1830 according to plans by Karl Friedrich Schinkel.

New splendor: The synagogue in Mitte

Neue Synagogue Berlin

I5 *Oranienburger Strasse 28/30 (Mitte); Oranienburgerstrasse S-Bahn station; Tel. 28 40 13 16; Sunday through Thursday 10 a.m. to 6 p.m., Friday 10 a.m. to 2 p.m. Entry fee: DM 5*

Built by Eduard Knoblauch, his son Gustav, and Friedrich August Stühler (1800 – 1865). Today the synagogue lies in the middle of Mitte's increasingly strong Jewish community.

Russian Orthodox Church

9D *Hohenzollerndamm 166 (Wilmersdorf); Fehrbelliner Platz S-Bahn station; Tel. 873 16 14; services Saturday 10 a.m. and 6 p.m., Sunday 10 a.m.*

A very beautiful church with five towers and the typical onion domes.

Berliner Dom (Berlin Cathedral)

J6 *Am Lustgarten (Mitte); Friedrichstrasse S-Bahn station; Tel. 20 26 91; Predigtkirche/Fürsten-gruft: Monday through Saturday 10 a.m. to 6 p.m., Sunday 12 noon to 6 p.m.*

This Evangelical church was built in the period between 1894 and 1905, according to an imperial decree by Kaiser Wilhelm II. The plans for the neobaroque structure were drawn up by the architect Julius Carl Raschdorff. The church lies on the site of a former cathedral.

Königin Elisabeth Kirche

J4 *Invalidenstrasse 3 (Mitte); Rosenthaler Platz subway station; Tel. 449 00 86; daily 9 a.m. to 5 p.m.*

Beautiful building by the architect Karl Friedrich Schinkel. The church does not have a tower, but its columns have a powerful uplifting effect.

Stattreisen

G2 *Malplaquestrasse 5 (Wedding); Tel. 455 30 28; cost: about DM 15 per person.*

Walks through the city with an emphasis on culture and history. An interesting range of themes, including Jewish Berlin and a tour that retraces the steps of Franz Biberkopf, hero of the classic novel Berlin Alexanderplatz.

Stadtverführung

K3 *Greifenhagener Strasse 62 (Prenzlauer Berg); Tel. 444 09 36; DM 14 per person.*

A whole range of tours featuring culture, museums, and architecture. Individual tours can also be arranged.

Frauentouren

K11 *Warthestrasse 50 (Neukölln); Tel. 626 16 51; 15 – 25 DM per person.*

Historical tours from a female perspective, for example: "Women Laborers in Prenzlauer Berg," and "Jewish Women and Resistance."

Fahrradstation

J5 *In the Hackesche Höfe, Rosenthaler Strasse 40 (Mitte); Hackescher Markt S-Bahn station; Tel.: 28 38 48 48; prices from DM 20.*

City tours by bike; you can bring your own or rent one here. Themes include architecture, history, and Berlin culture. There are also day tours into the countryside outside Berlin.

Extratouren

K8 *Lausitzer Strasse 13 (Kreuzberg); Tel.: 612 77 27; prices from DM 200, divided among the participants; 3-hour tours.*

Specializes in historical tours. Very informative biographical tours about Käthe Kollwitz and Rosa Luxemburg.

Day trips

Kloster Chorin (Chorin Monastery)

Chorin. *Go to Bernau S-Bahn station, then take the regional train to the Kloster Chorin station; if you're going by car, take the B2 past Bernau toward Eberswalde/Finow.*

Potsdam Film Museum: a unique story

This monastery of the Cistercian order was founded in 1273. It is located about fifty kilometers northeast of Berlin, surrounded by beautiful countryside. Large sections of the complex have been restored after years of decay. In autumn or winter the feeling here reminds one of the Umberto Eco novel, *The Name of the Rose.*

Werder

Werder *located 12 km west of Potsdam, on the Schwielowsee; Travel information available at the Werder tourist office, Tel. 03327/431 10.*

An island town full of beautiful gardens, with the atmosphere of a fishing village. Werder is located in the middle of the largest fruit-growing region in the eastern part of Germany. It's especially lovely to visit when the trees are in bloom.

Spreewald

Gross-Wasserburg. *Go to Königs-Wusterhausen S-Bahn station, take the train to Halbe, then ride a bicycle to Gross-Wasserburg.*

Beautiful lowlands with sandflats and dunes. Venice in the woods, writer Theodor Fontane said of the landscape. It's best to take a bicycle and come on a weekday, since the area becomes overcrowded on the weekends. You can also take a rowboat to Schlepzig (Unterspreewald).

Surrounding areas

Schloss Babelsberg (Babelsberg Castle)

Potsdam. *In Babelsberg Park; Babelsberg S-Bahn station; Tel. 0331/969 42 00; daily 10 a.m. to 5 p.m.; closed Mondays, open only on weekends in fall and winter; entry: DM 4.*

This neogothic castle, located in Potsdam's second-biggest park, was built by Karl Friedrich Schinkel from 1833 to 1835. Wonderful views of the Tiefer See and the Glienicker Lanke.

Filmpark Babelsberg

Potsdam *Entrance on Grossbeerenstrasse; Babelsberg S-Bahn station; Tel. 0331/721 27 50; daily 10 a.m. to 6 p.m.; entry: DM 28.*

Stunts, animal tricks, an

original film set from Das Boot, and much more.

Schloss Sanssouci (Sanssouci Castle)

Potsdam Potsdam Stadt S-Bahn station + Bus 606 or 695; Tel. 0331/969 42 00 ; Tuesday through Sunday 9 a.m. to 4 p.m.; entry DM 10.

Rococo castle in the middle of an enormous park (290 hectares). The castle was the summer residence of the Prussian king Frederick II. Almost all of the buildings are open to the public. Call to ask for tour times.

Glienicker Park

Wannsee Königstrasse, before the Glienicker Bridge, Wannsee S-Bahn station; Tel.: 805 30 41.

The park around the Kleinglienicke castle was created from 1824 to 1860. The Erlebnisgarten (Experience Garden) is a work of art.

Botanical Garden

Dahlem Königin-Luise-Strasse 6-8; Bus 101, 148, 183; Tel. 83 00 60 ; daily 9 a.m. to 8 p.m. (May through August, closes earlier at other times of year); entry: DM 6.

One of Europe's most beautiful botanical gardens, with a wide range of different species. Built between 1897 and 1910. The complex covers forty-two hectares and offers plenty of wide-open space for recreation.

Great minds rest in the east

Even immortals have to be buried someday.

Berlin has 190 cemeteries, which are nice places to go for a walk or to see the graves of famous people. Marlene Dietrich is buried in the Third City Cemetery (3. Städtischer Friedhof). Berlin's traditional cemeteries are located in Mitte. One of these is the Jewish Cemetery, which was leveled by the Nazis. The Berlin Wall used to go right through the Invalidenfriedhof (Invalid Cemetery), which at one time was the Prussian Heldenfriedhof (Cemetery of Heroes). Some stones still remain. Most of Berlin's famous intellectuals—Fichte, Hegel, Schinkel, Heinrich Mann, Bertold Brecht, and Heiner Müller—are buried in the Dorotheenstädtischer and Friedrichwerderscher Cemeteries, both of which are located in the east. The graves of revolutionaries Rosa Luxembourg and Karl Liebknecht are in Zentralfriedhof Friedrichsfelde.

3. Städtischer Friedhof (Third City Cemetery)

D9 Stubenrauchstrasse 43-45 (Schöneberg); Tel. 78 76 29 61.

Invalidenfriedhof

H 4/5 Scharnhorststrasse 33; daily 7 a.m. to 7 p.m.

Friedrichswerderscher Friedhof

I5 Chausseestrasse 126; daily 8 a.m. to 8 p.m.

Jüdischer Friedhof (Jewish Cemetery at Weissensee)

M3 Herbert-Baum-Strasse 45 (Mitte); Tel. 282 23 27; Sunday through Thursday 8 a.m. to 5 p.m., Friday 8 a.m. to 3 p.m.

Zentralfriedhof Friedrichsfelde

Friedrichsfelde; Gudrunstrasse; Tel. 559 75 33. Open all day.

Paris chic: At *Le Train Bleu*
everyone understands that
Paris was the only place where
Louis XIV could feel at home.

Paris

How can a single city be the
world capital of love, fashion, and multiculturalism?
The answer in bookstores this
November.

The nightlife in
Paris is an
expensive
pleasure, but
it never
disappoints.

Publishing Information

Publisher: te Neues Publishing
Editor-in-Chief: Anke Degenhard
Art Director: Kerstin Peters
Director of Photography:
Kerstin Richter
Editors: Christoph Becker (Manager),
Dirk Krömer
English edition: Umbrage Editions,
New York
Editor: Nan Richardson
Associate Editor: Xenia Cheremeteff
Art Director: Francesca Richer
Editorial Assistants: Anna Nordberg,
Laurent Gorse
Writers: Sonja Beckmann, Arne
Boecker, Oliver Gehrs, Sebastian
Holweg, Dirk Krömer, Matti Lieske,
Felix Neunzerling, Jürgen Sorges, Gayle
Tufts, Frédéric Ulferts, Caroline von der

Tann, Ralf Wollheim, Helmut Ziegler
Design: Barbara Sullivan, Christian
Bretter, Notburga Stelzer (Manager)
Berlin Editor: Luiza Boutasfat, Jörg
Lehmann (Photos), Karl-Heinz
Lubojanski (Manager)
Collaboration: AKW, Daniela Aue,
Tina Gangloff, Miriam Hanke, Nicole
Kleinfeld, Melina Schmidt, Markus Weber
Editorial address: Max City Guide,
Milchstrasse 1, 20148 Hamburg
Publisher's Address:
te Neues Publishing Company
16 West 22nd Street,
New York, NY 10010
Tel. 212-627-9090 Fax 212-627-9534
eMail: tnp@teneues-usa.com
www.teneues.com
MAX CITY GUIDE is a trademark of
the MAX Verlag GmbH & Co. KG.

The paperback edition of MAX CITY
GUIDE in English is a licensed edition
of the German magazine MAX CITY
GUIDE, published by agreement
between MAX Verlag GmbH & Co. KG,
a division of the publishing group
MILCHSTRASSE, Milchstrasse 1, 20148
Hamburg / Germany and te Neues
Publishing Company.
While we strive for utmost precision
in every detail, we cannot be held
responsible for any inaccuracies,
neither for any subsequent loss or
damage arising.

teNeues
www.teneues.com

The Max City Guides
also available as calendars

WALL CALENDARS
Size 30 x 30 cm
New York
ISBN: 3-8238-**3579**-3
London
ISBN: 3-8238-**3580**-7
Berlin
ISBN: 3-8238-**3581**-5
$12.99   c$19.50

Hot addresses for:
Clubs, Bars, Restaurants,
Hotels, Shopping,
Fitness, Internet.
With detachable map.

DELUXE DIARIES
Size 16.5 x 21.6 cm
New York
ISBN: 3-8238-**3696**-X
London
ISBN: 3-8238-**3697**-8
Berlin
ISBN: 3-8238-**3698**-6
$13.99   c$21.00

teNeues

 max City Guide **95**